CRUISING THROUGH FRANCE

Cruising Through France
with the Bermuda II

by
Tony Davis

The Pentland Press
Edinburgh – Cambridge – Durham – USA

First published in 1995 by
The Pentland Press Ltd
1 Hutton Close,
South Church
Bishop Auckland
Durham

ISBN 1-85821-301-0

Typeset by Carnegie Publishing, 18 Maynard St, Preston
Printed and bound in Great Britain by Bookcraft (Bath) Ltd.

To Antoinette
with love and thanks
and without whose daily journal
this book would not have been possible.

ACKNOWLEDGEMENTS

The aerial photograph of St Jean-de-Losne on page 135 is reproduced by kind permission of the photographer, M. Charles Gérard of H_2O Marina company.

The author wishes to acknowledge the assistance, advice and enthusiasm of Sasha and Eugene 'Penny' Simmons since the inception of the idea; Mrs Marjorie Cohen for keeping track of our whereabouts and forwarding countless bundles of mail; and the VP9 amateur radio operators for keeping us up-to-date with news from home.

CONTENTS

Intrusion

by Hugh McKnight

Tony Davis insists that I am in part to blame for this book. It seems that he and Antoinette might never have plunged into their extended foray through Europe's inland waterways if they had not been infected with enthusiasm from my own canal and river writings. Regularly, I receive letters from similarly affected strangers on the lines of: 'You have completely changed the lives of my wife and myself.' To be thus responsible for otherwise balanced adults departing from a stable existence 'on land' and becoming wandering gipsies is a curious sensation, as my own European waterways exploration (now dating back to the late 1960s) has mostly been achieved in small doses of a few weeks at a time. To maintain a much-loved house and garden and the necessity of earning a living prevent me from being afloat for eight months of the year. But how I envy those whose circumstances enable them to achieve just that!

I have seen many cruise accounts, all vainly searching for a publisher. For the greater part they were a dull collection, adding little to the literature of the subject. This book is quite different and can confidently find a place on the shelf alongside John Liley, Weston Martyr, George Millar and Roger Pilkington.

Tony and Antoinette Davis penetrated this world with few special skills or qualifications. Gradually they learned to cope with the occasional threatening *péniche* or lock keeper; with ill-tempered generators; and with the sometimes daunting intricacies of the French language. Nothing we read here is (or needed to be) exaggerated; canal life is every bit as fascinating as described by Tony Davis.

One day, this book will be regarded as a valuable social document, for European waterways are changing fast: more now than at any time in the last two centuries. Commercial freight traffic inexorably declines while pleasure boating continuously expands. And yet, the magic persists. I prefer not to regard such travel as 'boating' in the accepted sense: more, it is a wonderfully relaxing method of discovering a real backdoors France from aboard your floating home. My own *Avonbay* has long been considered an aquatic *maison secondaire* par excellence.

If, when you have read this thought-provoking book (which itself is surely destined to change more than a few lives) you feel inclined to emulate Tony and Antoinette Davis, I suggest you do not hesitate. Unless, perhaps, you first take the sensible route and rent a boat just to make certain that this is the life for you.

In these pages, there is evidence of a greatly-to-be-envied slow pace. Arrive at a new town or village, like it a lot and stay there for the next week—or two. Perhaps, one day, I'll be able to do that as well.

Years ago, I was one of several guests aboard a very large and very splendid motor yacht. Our host, a prominent British politician, was enormously proud of the fact that he had once cruised from the Mediterranean to the English Channel in slightly under three weeks. It appeared from present progress that he was intent on beating his own record. The guests breathed a sigh of relief when the owner went ashore on the Canal latéral à la Loire, mounted the ship's motor bike and raced up the towpath in a cloud of dust to ensure that the next lock would be ready for us. We throttled back and for the first time in several days noticed that we were no longer throwing a breaking wave onto the banks. We consequently took rather longer to reach the lock than expected and were greeted by our irate captain who had been awaiting our arrival for a full five minutes: 'Where the hell have you been? What do you think I'm doing this for? For fun?'

The Davis mentality *is* to cruise for fun. Sit back and relax as you savour their gentle meander through the French waterways. I know you'll enjoy it.

Hugh McKnight
The Clock House,
Shepperton-on-Thames.

ILLUSTRATIONS

MAPS

PROLOGUE

FRANCE

July 1977

'Not too close to the edge now, Michael!' Antoinette called out.

The youngster turned around, and with an exaggerated and theatrical 'bunny hop' moved back from the edge of the low, stone quay. The searing heat of the Mediterranean sun beat down on us as we stood on the quayside of the small town of Marseillan. From behind us, the unmistakable aroma of *soupe de poisson*, heavily laced with garlic, wafted from the kitchens of the very popular Hôtel du Port as the chef prepared for the regular lunchtime clientele. Beyond us, the metal pilings of the oyster beds in the Etang de Thau, shimmered in the midday sun. A few small sailing dinghys, their sails limp and lifeless, dotted the surface of the seventeen-kilometre long salt water lake.

'Come and take a look at this boat, Michael,' I said, taking our son's hand, in order to steer him away from the edge of the quay.

'I won't fall in, Dad. Anyway, I can swim.' he said petulantly.

'It's not that. Mum says that you only have enough clean clothes to last until we return home.'

We turned to the large Dutch motor cruiser that was moored against the quay. The paintwork glistened in the sunlight, and through the lightly tinted saloon windows, we could see a vase of fresh cut flowers in the centre of a highly polished wood table.

'Wouldn't it be fantastic to spend a couple of years just cruising around on the French canals in a boat like this?' I remarked.

'Dream on, Captain!' said Antoinette. 'When would we ever have the time or the money?'

From behind us, came an excited shout.

'Tony! Do you want some oysters for lunch?'

I turned around to see my brother-in-law carrying a bright red bucket that came from our hired cruiser. The bucket was full to the brim with huge grey-black oysters.

'I've got some lemons too, and a bottle of chilled white wine. Come on! Let's go.'

I cast one last appreciative and thoughtful glance at the cruiser before following my brother-in-law the length of the quay to our hire boat. We were having a wonderful family holiday, which, as always, had flown by far too quickly, but the boat that we had hired for two weeks cruising on the Canal du Midi, was a far cry from the Dutch cruiser.

I was still deep in thought as I slid the oyster knife under the shell of the first plump oyster.

The dream had begun.

Chapter 1

AMSTERDAM

On June 25th 1990, the dream came true.

Antoinette and I stood quietly in the June sunlight looking at what was to be our home for the next two years. Behind us, the Van der Vliet boat yard, located in Muiden on the outskirts of Amsterdam, was bustling with activity. In front of us lay a sleek, fifty foot, blue and white, trawler-style motor yacht. She nestled comfortably in the berth alongside the River Vecht and tugged gently at her mooring lines as if anxious to be underway. We had named her the *Bermuda II* and she was all ours. Hardly believing that a 13-year-old ambition was about to come to fruition, I found myself reminiscing on how it had all come about.

After years of managing my father-in-law's art studio, we found ourselves the victims of our own success. At 78, my father-in-law was finding it increasingly difficult to keep up with the hectic pace and demands of the ever fickle tourist trade. The business had been financially rewarding, and we had paid off the house mortgage years previously. Our son's educational expenses were also a thing of the past.

Antoinette had a thriving music teaching practice which operated out of our living room almost every day of the week. Arriving home from the studio each day after work, I was frequently greeted by the sounds of a young student murdering the scale of E flat minor on the flute. I would beat a hasty retreat to my radio 'shack' located in the garage and take solace in talking to my amateur radio friends around the world.

In addition to our working day, we found ourselves getting more and more involved in various voluntary organizations, to the extent that quite often we would have just an hour or so together over dinner, before one of us had to rush off to attend a meeting or a function somewhere on the island. It was time for a change.

One evening, in December 1989, over yet another rushed meal, the subject of France and the canals came up.

'Let's go to France,' I said.

'What, you mean for another holiday on the canals?' Antoinette responded. Over the past few years we had returned to France, time and time again, for a series of enjoyable holidays on the inland rivers and canals.

'No. I mean for an extended period. You remember that boat in Marseillan?'

'Yes. You're right,' she said slowly and thoughtfully. 'Now, might be a good time to do it. Perhaps we should look into it and give it some more serious thought,' she concluded, as she rushed off to yet another orchestral rehearsal.

We spent the next few weeks agonizing over the practicality of living on a boat for an extended period of two years or more, and what it would mean to give up the house which had been our home for the past fifteen years. Antoinette firmly insisted that if we were going to do it, the boat would have to be large enough so that we could live in comfort, and small enough that it could be handled by just the two of us. She also insisted that we consider such necessary creature comforts as a washing machine, a deep-freeze, and some method of keeping the boat warm in the winter months.

Early in the New Year I flew to England, and spent a frustrating two weeks looking at both new and secondhand boats that were advertised in the popular boating magazines. Many of them came close, but not one came within our fairly stringent specifications. In order safely to navigate on the smaller French canals, the boat would have to be restricted to a maximum draft of 1.80 metres, a beam of 5.0 metres and a head height of 3.50 metres from the waterline. The maximum permitted length was 38 metres, the length of a standard French lock, and this was unlikely even to enter into the equation. Our holiday adventures, cruising on the French canals, had also taught us that passage through some of the smaller locks could be surprisingly turbulent. All too often we had heard the sickening crack

2

and crunch of fibreglass and wooden boats as they had been thrown around in the confines of a lock chamber. It was for this reason therefore that we had decided that a steel hulled craft would be the most suitable.

Prior to leaving Bermuda, I had made arrangements to fly on from England to Holland if my search in the UK had not been successful. The evening before my departure for Holland, I telephoned Antoinette, in Bermuda. Gloomily, I had given her the bad news of my search thus far, and asked her if she thought that it was worthwhile continuing on to Holland.

'You've made all the arrangements, and gone all that way. It would be crazy to return home now,' she advised me.

The very next evening, I called Antoinette from a hotel in Amsterdam in a totally different frame of mind.

'The Van der Vliet agency seems to know exactly what we are looking for. Already I've seen several boats that would be suitable,' I told her excitedly. 'However, there is one boat in the south of Holland that looks just the ticket. I have only seen the specification sheet and a few photographs, and unfortunately the boat is miles away. The owner's not available and time is running out for me to make my return flight.'

Reluctantly, I left Holland without seeing the boat that had kindled my interest, and I returned to Bermuda with only the usual brokers specification sheet to show for my efforts. It was not until April that we could make arrangements to view the boat and this time we both made the transatlantic trip.

The town of Roermond is snuggled hard up against the German border in south Holland and the cold, frosty weather that we found there was a marked change from the warmth and humidity of Bermuda. Bundled up in the warmest clothes that we possessed, we climbed out of the car in which Ad Van der Vliet had driven us down from Amsterdam.

From the outside the *Cornelia* appeared to be everything that we had hoped for. A large aft deck, with exterior steering position, held the promise of summer entertaining and cruising. The low profile main saloon, with its large windows and interior wheel position, seemed just about the right height to negotiate low bridges and to provide a comfortable position from which to helm the boat in rainy weather.

The forward deck, which was both well protected and uncluttered, rose in a graceful curve towards the bow.

The *Cornelia* was a Doggersbank 702A, constructed of steel and built in Holland in 1972. She was, we were assured by Ad, a classic Dutch built motor cruiser. Her vital statistics of 1.25 metres draught, 4.35 metres beam and head height of 2.80 metres, when the steadying sail mast had been lowered to a horizontal position on the aft deck, fitted neatly within our requirements. She was powered by two 120 hp Ford Lehman diesel engines, which gave her a top speed of around 12.5 knots and would therefore be able to handle the swiftest flowing rivers with comparative ease. A 6 kilowatt, rather old Onan generator, supplied 220 volt mains power for the occasions when shore power was not available. Ad told us that in addition to the mains power sockets, we would find dual 24 volt D.C. sockets throughout the boat that ran the everyday electrics such as lights and fans. This was supplied from two huge battery banks located in a separate compartment beneath the saloon floor.

We went aboard and were greeted by the owners as we entered the spacious saloon. The interior warmth was a pleasant surprise and we hastily shed our coats, as deep beneath our feet came the soft whine of the diesel fired central heating system. After we had inspected the interior from stem to stern, we realized that we would have to make a few changes for long term living on board, but we also knew that this was the boat that we had been looking for. A suitable financial deal was concluded, subject to survey, and we returned home to Bermuda to commence the laborious, but exciting task, of collecting and packing everything that we thought we might need for our new way of life.

When we informed our friends and family of our decision, half of them thought that we were crazy, and the other half said so! Only Michael, who had moved into his own apartment, and who was enjoying his new found independence, encouraged us in our decision to leave our cloistered environment and to pursue our dream.

*   *   *

I was transported from the past to the present, by Antoinette squeezing my hand.

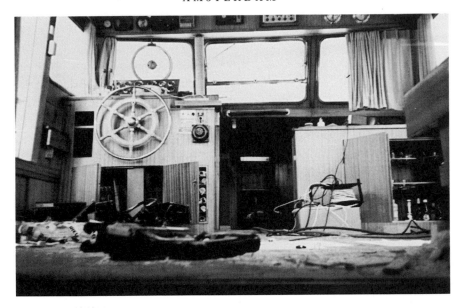

The interior was a mess.

'Let's go on board,' she said.

Taking the keys from my pocket, I unlocked the saloon door and slid it open. The interior was a mess. Electrical cables, pieces of pipe, wood and tools were littered everywhere. We gazed in disbelief at the scene of total chaos.

'Good heavens! They are nowhere near finished,' I said disappointedly. 'I had better find out what's going on.'

In April, we had left instructions regarding all the changes that we wanted to be done, and had planned to set out on our two year cruise through the inland waterways of Holland, Belgium and France by late June. We had requested that a small deep-freeze be installed in the middle cabin, the galley sink be moved to give more work space, a small fridge be incorporated in the galley under the counter top, and a washing machine/dryer combination unit was to be installed in the middle cabin. At the aft end of the saloon, we wanted a small wooden cupboard to house books. The top of the cupboard would double as a shelf for a stereo unit and my amateur radio equipment. It was evident that some work had been done on each of these projects, but I could not see how the work could possibly be completed in just four days.

The *Bermuda II* ready for launching.

The yard manager's office was located on the top floor of a large hangar-like building that overlooked the riverside moorings. Mounting the stairs, I found Wil Van der Linden busily working through some papers on his huge cluttered desk. It was the type of desk that should have a sign 'The Buck Stops Here' displayed in a prominent position, for it was Wil's responsibility to organize and oversee every detail of the work being carried out in the boat yard.

After the usual salutations and after the thick, dark, Dutch coffee had been poured, I quickly came to the point about the seemingly lack of progress that had been made on the boat. Wil, a great, gentle bear of a man, was as patient and as soothing as he had been on our previous visit to Holland in April. He assured me that all the work would be completed on time. I was not convinced, but I had a lot to learn about Dutch efficiency.

We had been staying at a small bed and breakfast guest house in Muiderberg, since our arrival in Holland and its close proximity to the boat yard was proving to be very convenient. Our friends Eugene and Sasha Simmons, together with their eldest son Scott, arrived from Bermuda, via Scotland, on Wednesday before our planned weekend departure, and moved into the Muiderberg guest house, with us. They had readily agreed to be our first guests, and to assist us with the shakedown cruise of the *Bermuda II*. Eugene, known to the world by his nickname of 'Penny' had just finished competing in the World International One Design sailing championships in Scotland where he had not been successful in repeating his winning form of the previous year.

There was not too much that we could do on the boat until the workmen had moved out, so we made good use of the time by visiting some of the many tourist attractions that Amsterdam has to offer. A trip around the centre of Amsterdam by canal boat, and a visit to the Rijks museum, were the highlights of our tourist itinerary. Penny and I went shopping for the appropriate inland waterway maps for our route south as far as the Belgium border, but despite searching in several chandlery shops we had no luck in obtaining the map that covered the Zuid Willemsvaart canal that was on our planned route south.

We dutifully purchased a copy of the *Almanak Voor Watertoerisme* which by law, has to be on board every boat that navigates in Dutch waters. The book is available only in Dutch and so for foreign yachts-men this law seems to be a pointless piece of legislation unless they can read Dutch.

As promised by Wil, the boat was ready for us to move into on Friday morning after having been hauled out of the water on Thursday afternoon, for a power washing and a coat of new anti-fouling on the bottom. At last we could unpack the china and personal belongings that we had airfreighted from Bermuda. As we were busily unpacking, a sign painter faithfully reproduced the Bermuda Coat of Arms on the bow of the boat. The Latin motto beneath the crest *Quo Fata Ferunt* (Where the fates may lead us) seemed particularly appropriate under the circumstances.

Despite our anxiety to move out of the guest house in Muiderberg where the obligatory hard boiled egg and cold meat platter for break-fast was getting a bit tedious, we quickly found out that we had so much work to do in stowing countless belongings, that we would need to spend one more night ashore before sleeping on the *Bermuda II* for the first time.

Arrangements were made with our bank in England to transfer telegraphically payment to the Van der Vliet boat yard for the work which had been carried out. We had been warned, in advance, that we would not be able to leave Muiden until the funds had arrived and had been cleared. I firmly believed that everything would be in order in a couple of days and that we would soon be on our way. My faith in the English banking system was completely shattered as it took several frustrating telephone calls over the next four days before we were finally informed that the funds had arrived and that we were now clear to depart.

On Thursday night we treated ourselves to an excellent dinner at the 'Doelan' restaurant overlooking the lock in Muiden. We were all in high spirits, and even the light rain that had started to fall could not dampen our enthusiasm as we walked back to the *Bermuda II* discussing, with high expectations, our adventure that was at long last to begin in the morning.

After we had all retired to our beds for the night, not a sound could be heard other than the gentle lapping of the water against the hull. I was on the verge of slipping into a sound sleep, when I was rudely awakened by a high pitched siren-like sound that seemed to be coming from the forward area of the boat. I had no idea what it was, but one thing was for certain—it appeared to be closer to Penny and Sasha's cabin, in the bow, than ours. My first thought was that it might be some device that Penny and Sasha had brought on board with them. If that was the case, then they would fix it soon enough. The howling continued incessantly. Pulling on a pair of shorts I made my way forward to the galley where I was quite surprised to see Penny crawling around on all fours.

'What the hell is that noise?' I shouted over the ear piercing racket.

'I don't know, but I think it's the gas alarm,' he shouted back. I had no idea where the gas alarm was situated but I did recall asking Fred the mechanic, to install one. By now, we were both crawling around on all fours, and we eventually located the offending object on the floor behind the gas stove. I violently jerked the two wires from the back of the device. If there is any such thing as a deafening silence, this was it.

'Crikey! What a damn silly installation. No switch, no button to turn it off, no reset button, nothing. Do you smell any gas Penny?' I asked nervously.

'No. Probably a malfunction. Better have Fred check it out in the morning.'

With an uneasy sigh of relief, I returned to the aft cabin and assured Antoinette that we were in no imminent danger of either sinking or blowing up. Once again, I climbed into my bunk, and this time the gentle lapping of the water against the hull lulled me into a peaceful, and uninterrupted sleep.

THE
ROUTE
SOUTH

North
Sea

Germany

Amsterdam

Utrecht

Netherlands

Lek

Waal

Maas

Zuid Willemsvaart

Köln

Helmond

Antwerp

Rhein

Maasbracht

Albert Canal

Maastricht

Belgium

Liege

Meuse

Koblenz

Germany

Givet

Luxembourg

Pont à Bar

Canal des Ardennes

Canal de l'Est

France

Verdun

Chapter 2

MUIDEN TO UTRECHT
38 KILOMETRES, 2 LOCKS

July 6th 1990

After all the waiting of the past few days, we were anxious to leave Muiden. We bade farewell to Ad Van der Vliet, and to Rachel, his second in command, who had done a lot to help us with our domestic purchases, Fred the mechanic, and all the other boatyard workers. A special farewell was said to Wil, who had not only become a good friend, but was, by now, more like a father figure to us.

We backed the *Bermuda II* gingerly, into the murky waters of the River Vecht and headed for the first lock, less than 200 metres away. We did not know it at the time, but we would pass through another 949 locks of various shapes, sizes and degrees of difficulty before we would see Muiden again.

Most of the locks in Holland, are very gentle affairs with less than a metre or two of rise and fall and they are operated with typical Dutch efficiency, the lock keepers stacking the locks to their liking in the interests of safety and convenience for the water borne traffic. Our first locking experience aboard the *Bermuda II* was accomplished in an unspectacular fashion.

The River Vecht was in a sombre mood, matching the overcast sky and incessant drizzle. It was also quite cold. If this was July in Holland, then I wanted to get to France just as soon as we could. We passed through the town of Weesp, and our first lifting bridge, of which there must be thousands in the Netherlands. A wooden clog, suspended from a fishing pole was swung out over the boat by the bridge keeper from

11

his control cabin. Obediently, we put some small change into the clog which was rapidly retrieved by the bridge keeper. The practice of tipping is not compulsory and we noticed many Dutch craft passing through and ignoring the bridge keeper's 'fishing' antics.

The town of Loenen had some convenient moorings quite close to the town centre so we stopped for lunch and did some leisurely grocery shopping before proceeding on our way, some two hours later.

That afternoon, we cruised between immaculate houses whose well kept lawns swept down to the river's edge. Colourful displays of white, pink and blue hydrangea bushes in full bloom tried their best to cheer up the gloomy day. Small boats of every description bobbed gently in our passing wake, each boat tied to a dock at the foot of flawless green lawns.

The landscape was as flat as an ironing board, and only now could we begin to understand why Holland has more bicycles per capita than any other nation on earth. No hills to struggle up here. I found myself smiling, once again, at Fred's little joke when he had mischievously told us that he was off to the Dutch mountains for the weekend. Now and again we would pass the occasional windmill, a reminder of times past, when they were used extensively to pump water from the low-lying land and to prevent the polders from being reclaimed by the sea. Today, modern pumping stations controlled by computer technology have made most of the windmills redundant, although a few still carry out their historic duties.

That night, we found quiet moorings about 150 metres upstream from the lifting bridge that carries the main road into the centre of the town of Maarssen. Dinner that evening was in a small, but pleasant, Italian restaurant.

The next day was Saturday and, clad in our boating rain suits, we explored the little town with its interesting seventeenth-century houses where each pane of glass sparkled like a jewel in defiance of the cloudy conditions. It was market day, and it appeared that the entire town was out shopping and looking for bargains. In one of the cobbled main streets, children had set up individual stalls and were busy selling off their used toys and books for charity, re-cycling Dutch style. A marching band added to the happy, carnival atmosphere of this picturesque Dutch town.

Despite the rain, we decided to continue cruising towards Utrecht

Approaching the first bridge in Utrecht.

that afternoon, as time was running out for Penny and Sasha who had an early morning flight from Amsterdam booked for Sunday.

Arriving on the outskirts of Utrecht, we were faced with two choices. We could either go out on to the Amsterdam–Rijn canal, or continue on the River Vecht and go straight through the centre of Utrecht. After a little deliberation, we decided on the latter, as we did not want to participate in the free-for-all on the Amsterdam–Rijn canal where barges in excess of 6,000 tons plough by at great speed in both directions.

At the first lock, before the city of Utrecht, we lowered the mast and dismantled the windscreen panels in front of the aft steering position and we asked the lock keeper if it was possible for a boat the size of *Bermuda II* to get through all the old bridges.

'What is your head-height?' he inquired, casting a critical and professional eye over the *Bermuda II*.

'Two metres eighty.'

'Yes, it is possible,' he decreed in that guttural way of speaking English that the Dutch have.

We passed through the lock and after a short distance we came to the first red brick bridge. I looked with alarm at the narrow and impossibly low arched brickwork. Turning to Penny, who was on the wheel, I could see that he, too, was looking at the opening with some apprehension.

Very slowly we moved forward and slid the bow into the centre of the opening. As we went under the bridge, Penny made a slight misjudgment and twelve inches of varnish was stripped from the starboard aft rail as it brushed against the curved brickwork. At the next bridge, we were positioned exactly right and with Penny stooping low at the controls on the aft deck steering position, we made it through safely.

By this time, we had gathered quite a following of onlookers who were intrigued to see a boat the size of *Bermuda II* attempting this tricky passage through the centre of Utrecht. The onlookers would gather on the bridge above us and they would watch as the bow went under the bridge. Once the bow was under, they would then rush across the road to the other side and watch expectantly as we came out, checking the boat's superstructure to see if we had left anything behind as we came through.

Utrecht is a marvellous city with interesting seafaring traditions and we were now passing through the old section of the city where disused waterside wharves and warehouses had been converted into chic restaurants, clubs and bars.

The waterway became narrower. The red-bricked buildings, covered in green slime at the waterline, seemed to press even closer to *Bermuda II* and her pristine dark-blue hull. The bridges became more like tunnels and the pigeons roosting up under the roofs were less than happy with our intrusion. At our approach they flew out in droves. This only added to Penny's discomfort as he had to duck and weave in order to avoid their panic stricken flight and their fear induced bombing runs.

On more than one occasion, we startled busy chefs by peering into their kitchens through grimy canalside windows through which they would not normally expect to be scrutinized in their daily work. Once they had overcome their surprise, the chefs' cheery waves did little to ease the mounting tension on board the *Bermuda II*.

Penny stooped lower and lower as the brickwork almost scraped his hands on the twin throttle controls. We were now finding out where the highest point was on the *Bermuda II* once the aft windscreen had been removed, and the mast laid flat on the rear anchor winch.

If another boat had been coming from the opposite direction, it would have been impossible for us to pass in the narrow confines of the waterway. I turned pale at the thought of having to back up. Going forward was difficult enough!

After the sixteenth bridge, we emerged into open water and made a right hand turn into the Singlegracht where we thankfully tied up alongside the wooden pontoon. It was still raining and the large trees under which we moored did nothing to diminish the downpour. I promptly dived below for a double Scotch, grateful that Penny, with his expertise in handling large boats at close quarters, had seen us safely through a very difficult and trying experience. I was finding out that cruising in one's 'house' evokes far more protective feelings than banging around the buoys in a racing sail boat.

Penny and Sasha left the boat to find out about travel arrangements for their early morning Sunday flight. After a short time, they returned to the boat and announced that they had found a taxi driver who was willing to drive them to Schipol airport in Amsterdam where they could easily obtain overnight accommodation at one of the airport hotels. The taxi was waiting alongside the boat with the meter running. While Sasha furiously crammed clothing into their roll bags, we exchanged hurried plans for the future. They would return next year and they were looking forward to spending more time cruising on the *Bermuda II* in European waters.

At 5.00 p.m. Penny and Sasha left the boat carrying their overstuffed roll bags. We were alone and except for the steady drip of rain on the deck above our heads, not a sound was to be heard. This was it. This is what we had come for. Had the sun been shining, we might have felt differently, but that night we could not help feeling slightly depressed, alone, vulnerable and far away from home, family and friends. We realized that from here on in, twenty-four hours a day, we would be responsible for each other's well being and that we would have to be our own electrician, plumber, mechanic, cook, housekeeper and physician.

After all the excitement of the past few days we were in a sombre mood that night.

Chapter 3

UTRECHT TO HELMOND
96 KILOMETRES, 11 LOCKS

July 8th/18th, 1990

I woke up slowly, vaguely registering that the soft sound of rain falling on the deck above my head had ceased sometime during the night. I could see that Antoinette was still sleeping peacefully in the bunk opposite. As I slid out from under the duvet, she stirred and turned over at the sound of my movements.

'What's the time?' she asked sleepily.

'9.30 a.m., would you believe!'

Two eyes sprang open. 'What? I didn't realize that it was so late.'

'Never mind. We have the whole day to ourselves. No telephones to answer, no visitors coming to the door, no disturbances of any kind. I'll go and put the coffee on,' I said, and made my way forward to the control console in the saloon. I prepared to activate the generator. Today we would have fresh brewed coffee from the electric coffee machine, as opposed to instant coffee which we both dislike intensely.

After holding down the pre-heat switch for the prescribed thirty seconds, I put the generator switch into the 'On' position and expected to be rewarded by the deep rumble of the generator coming to life beneath my feet. Nothing happened. Not a fizz, pop or whirr! I hurriedly checked that all the appropriate switches were in the correct position and tried again. Still nothing. I went down to the galley and put the kettle on the gas stove, resigning myself to instant coffee before investigating the generator malfunction further. I flicked on the switch to the overhead galley light intending to shed more light into the back

16

of the cupboard where I knew that the jar of instant coffee would be hiding.

The light did not come on. I realized then, that we had more of a problem than I had at first imagined, for not only was the generator not working but the battery power was also out of action.

I took a cup of coffee to Antoinette who was still snuggled in her bed and gave her the bad news that the *Bermuda II* was dead in the water with no electrical power whatsoever.

After a quick cup of coffee, I discovered to my horror, that both main battery banks were completely dry. I mentally kicked myself for having assumed that the batteries would have been inspected by the boat yard prior to our departure. Today was Sunday and it would be Monday before anyone would be in attendance at the Van der Vliet boat yard. With no battery, generator or shore power it was fortunate that we had not yet stocked the deep freeze with food. If we had done so the food would all have been defrosted by now.

I purchased several litres of distilled water from a nearby garage and dispensed it into the five thirsty batteries, and hoped that some residual charge would develop. It became apparent by late afternoon that we were stuck until we could get professional assistance from the boat yard in Muiden. So much for being our own electricians!

On Monday morning, I located a coin operated telephone box near to our mooring in the Singlegracht, and set about trying to contact either Wil or Ad Van der Vliet. After several unsuccessful attempts at depositing my coin into the box and not getting a dial tone, out of sheer frustration I walloped the side of the money collection box with the palm of my hand. To my surprise a cascade of coins fell around my feet from the return coin slot. The offending copper coloured Belgian coin that had jammed the mechanism stood out clearly from the bright silver coloured Dutch guilders. I pocketed my windfall and re-introduced the one guilder coin into the slot. I managed to make contact with Wil who was dismayed to hear of our predicament and promised that he would have Fred drive down later in the day with a set of replacement batteries.

I returned to the boat where I found Antoinette talking to a group of Dutch people who were holidaying on their own two small boats. They were concerned, and upset, that we had not asked for their assistance the day before. They were very kind and despite my protestations that help was on its way, they insisted on seeing what they could do to help with the flat batteries. We learnt that the ringleader of the assistance group was a truck driver and, as befits a man of his profession, was a very burly character indeed. His wife, a rather diminutive person was exactly the opposite, and she informed us that she was an assistant in a mental hospital, which seemed an appropriate occupation for what was about to take place.

Our truck driver friend hefted single handed, an ancient, World War II, army surplus, petrol-powered generator, and set it up on the dockside with the aim of charging our battery banks. After everyone had pulled and tugged on the starter cord, almost to the point of exhaustion, the generator still failed to start. This was probably just as well as the carburettor leaked so badly that I was sure that the whole thing would explode the instant it started. By now the water beneath the pontoon was slicked with a rainbow of petrol and Antoinette rushed around the assembled multitude advising them not to smoke.

We were eventually saved from impending disaster when Fred arrived early with a set of new batteries in the back of his van. The batteries were large heavy-duty monsters and it took two of us to carry them, one at a time, from the van to the boat. It took Fred about an hour, working with a hacksaw, and ample advice from our truck driver friend, to make a few alterations to the battery compartment before the new batteries could be safely put into place. Much to our relief, and a clap on the shoulder from our new found friend that almost took my breath away, the twin diesel engines roared into life, at last.

Fred then turned his attention to the generator but in spite of his best efforts he was unable to get the generator to start. It was therefore not a battery problem but something a little more serious. He told us that he would make arrangements for a mechanic from the Onan factory to come to the boat and sort out the problem. In the evening, Wil arrived at the boat, and after a brief investigation he located a fractured connection on the starter motor which was the cause of the malfunction. Wil stayed for a drink before leaving us and assured us that the Onan mechanic would quickly be able to repair the generator in the morning.

The next morning, the Onan mechanic confirmed Wil's diagnosis but on searching through all the spares that he carried in his van could not find the correct size of nut that was required to complete the job.

He ended up making a round trip of sixty kilometres to the main Onan repair facility in Gouda - all for the sake of a half inch nut.

The generator rumbled into life shortly after lunchtime and once again all systems were in working order on board the *Bermuda II*.

Leaving Utrecht the next day, complete with a miniature pair of blue and white Dutch clogs which were suspended in the wheelhouse and which were a gift from the truck driver's wife, we headed down the busy Merwede Canal to Gorinchem. Prior to our departure, we had arranged that my cousin who lives in England, would act as our mail 'clearing house' and would forward batches of mail to selected poste restante facilities along our route. Gorinchem was to be our first mail pick up point. The Merwede Yacht Club made us feel very welcome, and as the weather had improved considerably we did not mind the four day wait for the mail to arrive.

The Merwede Yacht Club flies courtesy flags from the yardarm of the club's flag pole indicating the different nationalities of the visiting craft. The large Bermuda flag that we flew had them confused, but we were pleased to see a red ensign being run up as our courtesy substitute.

After four pleasant days of glorious sunshine, we left Gorinchem and headed south on the Zuid Willemsvaart Canal, which is a great concrete ditch cut through uninspiring countryside with nothing of any interest to relieve the monotony.

We made a brief overnight stop in the sleepy little town of Ammerzoden and we had hoped for a couple of days in s'Hertogenbosch to visit the magnificent Gothic cathedral. The cathedral houses a collection of paintings by Hieronymus Bosch, one of the most famous Dutch painters of the fifteenth century. However, much to our dismay we could not find a suitable mooring and so we reluctantly continued on our way south.

By late afternoon we were getting quite concerned about finding a mooring for the night. The concrete sloping sides of the canal offered no chance of a safe mooring spot. Our plight was further hampered because we were using a road map for navigating purposes as all of our efforts to purchase the canal map covering the waterway had been in vain.

At 9.00 p.m. we still had not found a stopping place, and we decided that the small Dutch cruiser ahead of us would be facing the same

Close encounters at Helmond.

problem. Hoping that he knew where he was going, we followed closely behind, watching his every move.

Just as the late evening twilight gave way to darkness, the cruiser made an abrupt left hand turn into a small side canal dominated by tall grain silos. We followed him like a cat after a mouse.

Upon entering the small canal, we were relieved to see a number of vacant mooring spaces alongside a tree-lined bank that was directly opposite a large factory. It was not exactly the perfect place to spend the night but we were both so tired that it mattered little to us. After a quick, light supper we fell exhausted into our bunks.

We needed no alarm clock to rouse us early the next morning, as the factory opposite the boat sprang into noisy action shortly before 7.00 a.m. We took advantage of the enforced early morning wake up call by getting underway, and by lunchtime we were moored in a busy section of the canal in the town of Helmond.

The designated mooring basin was surprisingly located in a narrow section of the canal between two lifting bridges. The width of the canal allowed for single lane traffic only to pass in either direction close to the starboard side of the *Bermuda II*. We were still very new to inland navigation and the steady procession of large barges passing within a few metres of the boat was a constant source of interest, and at times a cause for some concern.

We were situated within a couple of hundred metres from a very large modern supermarket, which gave us the convenience of being able to push a laden supermarket trolley right up alongside the boat. For the first time we were able to provision the boat completely, and with comparative ease, so we took advantage of the situation by stocking up on Long Life milk, juice and canned goods. Strangely enough, up until now, we had not seen much fresh fish for sale in Holland, but this supermarket had a wonderful display of every imaginable seafood. We stocked the deep freeze with a few salmon steaks and some Dover Sole, as our diet of chicken, pork and ham had been getting a little repetitive. Antoinette is a real 'island girl' and loves any fish cooked in a variety of ways. That night we treated ourselves to fresh plaice expertly prepared by Antoinette in our small, but efficient galley. This was more like the lifestyle we had imagined, and already the tricky passage through Utrecht and the inconvenience of the electrical problems, were fast fading from our memories.

Chapter 4

HELMOND TO GIVET
204.2 KILOMETRES, 27 LOCKS

July 20th/31st, 1990

We did not stay long in Helmond. After two nights alongside, we cast off and continued our journey southwards towards Maastricht and the Belgium border. Our main objective was to leave Holland and Belgium fairly quickly and then to slow down and meander slowly southwards through France as the autumn approached.

We planned to stop for one night at the well equipped Koeweide Yacht Club near Maasbracht. This turned into three nights when we were enticed to stay longer by the availability of dockside water and mains electricity, which allowed us to catch up on the backlog of laundry that we had accumulated. This meant that not only could we leave with full water tanks but also we could avoid having the generator chugging away for hours on end. At the same time we made full use of the restaurant facility at the club and Antoinette had time off from cooking duties.

It turned out that we had made the right decision in taking advantage of the facilities in Koeweide, as our next overnight stop in Maastricht offered neither water or electricity. Had it not been for our desire to reach France quickly, we would have liked to investigate the town of Maastricht more fully, but we knew that we would be passing this way again at the end of our inland waterways cruising.

A short distance from Maastricht is the Belgium/Dutch border with the respective customs offices located inconveniently on opposite sides of the canal which leads to the Belgium controlled Lanaye Lock at the border. In order to retrieve the VAT which had been paid on the work and equipment used in fitting out the *Bermuda II*, the Van der Vliet boat yard had given me a form which was to be stamped by the customs officials at the border.

Upon reflection, I realized that I was foolish to approach the Belgium customs post first and to request that they stamp the form to certify that the boat had entered Belgium. The customs official readily took down the details concerning the *Bermuda II* which was tied up directly beneath his waterside office, and for a charge of 35 Belgian francs (60p) he handed me the Droits de Navigation form that was to be stamped by each lock keeper on our passage through Belgium. When confronted with the VAT form he shook his head and told me, in French, that I would have to get the form stamped by the Dutch authorities across the canal.

Casting off our mooring lines, we waited for a break in the convoy of barges that were rushing to get into the Lanaye lock. Half way across the waterway we had to weave in and out of the downstream convoy that, moments before, had been ejected from the lock and seemed anxious to finish their day's journey as far into Holland as they could possibly get. Having gained the comparative safety of the quay on the Dutch side, I scampered up the steps to the customs office and presented the VAT form. Despite my cajoling, the Dutch customs officer could not be persuaded to stamp the form and told me, in English, that the Belgium customs would have to do it. Holding the form at the top corner between finger and thumb, he handed it back to me as if it was some limp rag carrying a contagious disease.

We cast off our lines, and once again waited for a break in the commercial traffic and returned to the Belgium side of the canal. This time, sensing that all was not well with his counterpart on the other bank, the Belgium official stunned me by taking back the Droits de Navigation form that he had previously given me. The 35 Belgian francs that I had paid was not included in this transaction. He told us that we would get the form back once we had resolved the situation with the Dutch customs. I looked longingly at the telephone on his desk and asked, in very broken French, if he could call his counterpart whose office we could see through the window. Like a slow moving pendulum in a grandfather clock, he waved his forefinger from side to side in mid air. It was apparent that my request was totally out of the question, after all it was an international call and to spend the Belgian government's money in such a way was unheard of.

Once again, *Bermuda II* breasted the mighty six inch waves across 200 metres of international waters. Once inside the Dutch customs post, I insisted that the officer on duty, telephone a superior authority in order to obtain instructions on how to process the VAT reclamation form. Reluctantly, the officer reached for the telephone and after a brief exchange in Dutch he replaced the receiver and with a shrug, and a complete look of disgust on his face, dutifully stamped the form. Obviously, in his book, to obtain money back from the Dutch government was a heinous crime! However, he still did not give me back my copy of the precious form, and instead he sat gazing at the ceiling as if seeking divine guidance. Suddenly, a weak smile came across his face.

'You have to pay the tax somewhere,' he said slowly and purposefully, with his eyes lighting up, as the wisdom of his words hung in the air. This non-capitalist thought he had me.

'Ah! Yes, that will be in Bermuda then when we take the boat home,' I said, waving my new maroon coloured passport in the air. 'The tax is wicked there.' This was, of course, a complete and utter lie, as we have no taxes, as such, in Bermuda, and we had no intention of making a transatlantic trip in the *Bermuda II*. This information seemed to please him somewhat and he handed me back my copy of the document with a sly smile of the type that covertly says 'Gotcha!'

'Good practice, all this tying up and untying,' I said to Antoinette cheerfully on our fourth transit of the canal. My dry sense of humour was completely lost on her as she missed the bollard on the Belgian side in her attempt to lasso it with the bow line.

The Belgian customs officer smiled, and wished us *'Bon voyage'* as he handed me back the Droits de Navigation. After a short delay we were packed into the Lanaye lock with a variety of very large barges. We were the only pleasure boat in the lock and as such were relegated to the rear of the lock with just enough clearance between our stern davits and the aft lock gate. As the barges ahead of us churned out of the lock, we kept our lines firmly attached until the turbulence had subsided and we could safely make our exit from the lock.

We found the small pleasure port in Liège, between the Pont Kennedy and the Pont Albert, packed with various pleasure craft but there was just enough room for us to get alongside the wall opposite the protective arm that shields the moorings from the ever passing commercial traffic.

We had only been secured alongside for about fifteen minutes, when a voice from the wall above called down to us. 'What flag is that?'

I stood on the aft deck and looked up at an elderly gentleman, who was looking down at our Bermuda flag which was flying proudly from the stern flag pole.

'The Bermuda flag,' I said, happy to find an English speaking person in whom to confide our origins.

'Oh, I don't think that I have ever seen one of those. My name's Dick Hunt and that's my barge over there,' he said, indicating a 30 metre Luxemotor barge moored on the river side of the pleasure port. I had detected a slight Australian accent in Dick's speech and my feelings were confirmed when I noticed the Australian flag flying from the stern of the barge. We invited Dick on board, and over a gin and tonic, we found out that Dick and his wife, Jane, were in the hotel barge business and that they had been plying the inland waterways of Europe for quite some time. When we found out that Jane was off visiting friends for a few days, we invited Dick to stay and share dinner with us.

Antoinette produced some pork chops from the deep freeze and while they were defrosting, we cross-examined Dick about life afloat. He was a mine of information and we dug deeply into his first hand knowledge and experience. We were impressed, and slightly incredulous, to learn that Dick had worked his way through at least 3,000 locks, a figure which to us at the time, seemed almost unbelievable.

As Dick left us that night, he remarked that he had noticed that we were not flying the navigation flag from the pennant flag pole on our bow.

'The what?' I asked innocently.

'If you navigate in Belgium, you have to fly a red flag with a white rectangle on it from the bow of the boat.'

'Why's that?'

'Just part of the regulations,' he said. It suddenly dawned on me that we had indeed noticed the red and white flag on other craft but had naïvely thought that it was some sort of private yacht club, or some boating organizations burgee! We had not been told of this regulation and none of the resource books that we had on board had mentioned it.

The next morning, we giggled wickedly as Antoinette stitched two white face cloths on to both sides of the red international 'B' pennant that was taken from the boat's wardrobe of signal flags.

We visited Dick on board his barge the *Zeelands Luister* for morning coffee and were impressed with the size of the accommodations and the tastefully decorated interior. A pile of washing up in the sink silently testified that Jane was still off visiting friends!

For a couple of hours Dick patiently went through the canal maps for our journey south, marking suitable moorings and places of interest. Dick even went as far as to indicate the small town of St. Jean-de-Losne on the River Saône where we could get mechanical assistance should we require it on our way south. Antoinette scribbled down the name of the company H_2O, and the proprietor's name. We thanked Dick for all of his information and returned to the *Bermuda II* anxious to be off. We mounted our homemade navigation flag on the bow and received Dick's approval as we motored slowly past *Zeelands Luister* and headed upstream.

The next few days were spent cruising through the Ardennes region, and we were very impressed by the natural beauty of the scenery along the Meuse River valley. Heavily wooded slopes of coniferous trees intermingled with vast rust coloured cliffs and rocky crags. There was, however, a few eyesores. In some areas, large quarrying operations sent clouds of dust into the air, coating the trees in the immediate area with a film of grey dust.

Brief overnight stops in the towns of Namur and Dinant, both with excellent facilities for pleasure boats, whetted our appetites for a return visit some time in the future when we would have the time to explore fully each town. We were drawing ever closer to the French border at Givet and our longing to reach France precluded lingering for any length of time.

On Tuesday, July 31st, we left Dinant early. We took Dick Hunt's advice to top up our fuel tanks prior to our entry into France as he had told us that diesel fuel was far more expensive in France than in Belgium.

At 1.30 p.m. we crossed the border into France and moored outside the French customs post at Givet. The customs officer gave our

River Meuse—Ardennes, Belgium.

passports and ship's papers a cursory, bored look, as I placed them on the counter.

'Do you have any firearms on board your boat, Monsieur?' he asked in French. Receiving a negative reply, he rapped the edge of the documents on the counter top and waved a magnamanious hand indicating that we may proceed into France.

We were in high spirits, and once we had secured the boat alongside the stone quay reserved for pleasure boats, we walked around the town investigating the shops and searching for a restaurant in which to have a celebratory dinner. We had arrived in France. Apart from the problems in Utrecht and the day-long grind on the Zuid Willemsvaart without a canal map, we had made it in one piece. Our dream really was coming true.

We telephoned our son Michael in Bermuda, and he was delighted to hear of our progress, and that we had achieved our first goal of getting the boat safely from Holland to France. There was a tinge of envy in his voice as he wished us good luck on our continuing journey. We had faint pangs of guilt for having made him move out of the house in Bermuda to set up a life for himself in his own apartment. I was quickly consoled when he assured me by saying 'What you two are doing, is just great. You are doing something with your lives that other people just dream about. Don't worry about me, I am just fine.' He was right of course, and I silently thanked him for his understanding.

That evening, we celebrated our arrival in France by having a wonderful meal at the Restaurant Beaudoin where the food was superb and equal to our wildest expectations. We strolled back to the boat in the warm night air, elated at our progress to date. Later, two very happy people fell asleep in their bunks and looked forward to the morning when our journey through France would commence.

Chapter 5

GIVET TO VERDUN
203.1 KILOMETRES, 40 LOCKS

July 31st/August 12th, 1990

I was still in a buoyant mood when we woke up the next morning. The sun shone brightly from an azure blue sky and only a whisper of wind occasionally rippled the river's mirror-like surface.

A family of ducks paddled lazily past the boat and eagerly accepted half a crumbled baguette that was left over from lunch the previous day. Throughout our entire trip, Antoinette would never tire of feeding the ducks and the swans wherever we went.

Now that we had achieved our prime objective of getting the boat to France, I felt both of us beginning to relax, knowing that from this point on we could take our time and enjoy the towns and villages along our route.

It was not until 10.30 a.m. that we cast off our lines and pointed *Bermuda II* south towards the Canal de l'Est and the commencement of the French canal system. Up until now, we had been travelling on the River Meuse, whose wide breadth and large locks, had made for comfortable cruising. The locks on the Canal de l'Est, were of greatly reduced size and conformed to the dimensions suggested by the Freycinet Act of 1879, which established a minimum size for the French lock chambers. This Act allowed a standard 350 tonne *péniche* of 38.5 metres length, by 5.05 metres beam, to fit snugly into the lock chamber. The waterways, notably the Canal d'Orléans and the Canal du Berry, among others, which did not upgrade their locks to the new dimensions, eventually fell into a state of disuse and were declassified.

The approach to the Ham tunnel.

At the first lock, we were amazed at just how much water turbulence was created when the paddles of the upstream gate were opened. It seemed to be far more violent than what we could remember from our hire boat holidays on other French canals. As we rose up in the lock, we were pushed not backwards, as one might expect, but forward towards the upstream exit gates. The water cannoned off the rear gates and surged forward, taking us with it until the boat was checked by our stern line. Inexplicably, the boat would then surge backwards until checked by the bow line, each surge to and fro being more violent than the one before. We nicknamed this phenomena 'the dance of death' and it was not until we had passed through quite a number of locks that we learnt that the best way to counteract the surging was to make sure that the bow and stern lines were secured at right angles to the boat. That was the theory, at least, but invariably the lock bollards were positioned for large commercial craft and were therefore too far apart. We did learn that an additional rope admidships greatly reduced this uncomfortable surging.

We knew that after the first lock, we would have to pass through our first tunnel, the 565-metre-long Ham tunnel. Once through the lock, I broke out in a cold sweat as I looked at the extremely small opening that was the tunnel entrance. 'No way,' I thought to myself, as we slid ever closer to what appeared to be impending doom. Had I made a mistake in my research of the maximum permissible head height on the French canals? The prospect of retracing our voyage and having to tell all our friends that we had made a serious error in the size of boat that we had purchased, was not a pleasant thought. Cautiously and anxiously, I poked the bow of *Bermuda II* into the gloom of the tunnel. We could actually fit! Keeping the bow firmly fixed on the semicircular shaft of light that marked the other end of the tunnel, we proceeded very slowly. Although the interior of the tunnel was not lit, and the stone work was in need of some attention, we passed through without any problems.

Emerging into the bright sunlight, we only had a few moments to congratulate ourselves on this successful passage through our first ever canal tunnel, before passing through the next lock. After a short, man-made, canal cut we rejoined the welcome breadth of the River Meuse.

We passed through another five locks before mooring for the night in the town of Fumay. The mooring was a little precarious as the pleasure boat quay which was under construction had not yet been completed. I managed to boom out the stern of the boat with the metal pole that we carried on board for just such an event. By carefully positioning the four large fenders, I decided that we were reasonably safe for the night.

The heat of the day had subsided and a group of villagers were playing boules in the dusty gravel area which ran alongside the river bank. The game of boules is played everywhere, and with unrivalled passion, throughout France. Unlike English bowls, which requires a flat and impeccably kept grass playing surface, boules has the advantage that it can be played on any reasonably level surface. The metallic 'thunk' and 'click' of the balls in the gathering dusk, became a sound that would become very familiar to us over the next two years.

We decided that we would get a fairly early start the next day, mainly due to our precarious mooring arrangement, but also to allow us to cover as much ground as possible before the real heat of the day set in about 2.00 p.m.

After an early breakfast, we left Fumay shortly before 8.00 a.m. which for us, was indeed an early start! It was a time when the river valley was still enshrouded in a light mist which gave an ethereal look to the densely wooded slopes that defined the river's course.

With engines ticking over at less than half speed, we motored very slowly, not wanting to disturb the peace of such glorious scenery on such a lovely morning. The river was like a sheet of glass, disturbed only by a few fish jumping for an early morning snack of a passing flying insect. As the fish fell back into the water, the resulting ripples spread in perfect, undisturbed, concentric circles till they lapped gently at the reed beds at the river's edge. It was sheer bliss to glide along in such peaceful surroundings with not another living soul in sight.

We passed through three locks in quick succession before coming to the entrance of the 224-metre Revin tunnel. Being veterans of at least one tunnel passage, we were more relaxed and more confident, than on our first experience, only twenty-four hours previously!

At 11.30 a.m. we were in the narrow lock cut between locks 47 (Connune) and 46 (Deville) when suddenly a barge swept around the corner heading in our direction at great speed. The barge was in the centre of the canal and as it approached it became obvious that it was not going to give way one inch! As the barge came amidships, the water was sucked from the sides of the canal and the forward part of our keel touched bottom, and the stern was sucked towards the barge. I knew that we were going to hit. Frantically, I gunned the engines hoping to push us further in towards the bank but my efforts were in vain. With a resounding 'clang' the aft portside rubbing rail received a violent blow which swiveled the bow back into the centre of the canal. The barge continued on its way without slackening speed, and while we were still recovering from the shock, we heard shouts of panic and anger as the barge hit a small pleasure boat that was travelling about 100 metres astern of us.

The incident had shaken us up a bit, but our boat was undamaged. We were thankful that we had decided on a steel hulled boat for cruising on the inland waterways. *Bermuda II* had received her second battle scar, and apart from three inches of damaged white paint on the rubbing rail, all was well. At the next lock, my limited knowledge of French prevented me from having a meaningful conversation with the Belgian family who were travelling in the small boat behind us, and who were considerably upset by the whole affair.

It was a very hot day, and when the moorings at the town of

Monthermé came into view we decided to pull over for lunch and an afternoon siesta. Later, we were refreshed enough to continue on our way and we eventually reached the pleasure port in Charleville-Mézières just before 6.00 p.m.

Once we were moored up, I went below to the deep-freeze where Antoinette had the foresight to put a bottle of Eau Mineral, an hour earlier. I sat in the saloon and drank the whole litre bottle! We were used to the sun and humidity of Bermuda, but this was raw dry heat with no humidity. My skin felt like parchment.

Before leaving Bermuda, we had discussed the possibility of meeting up with Antoinette's sister, Joanne, and her husband, Sjur. They were hiring a cruiser from a boat base in Gray on the River Saône. After consulting the distance tables in David Edwards May's excellent guide *Inland Waterways of France*, I realized that it would mean that we would have to cover 340 kilometres, and transit 134 locks in about thirteen days. Allowing for the fact that the locks do not operate on Sundays in the southern branch of the Canal de l'Est, a leisurely, and comfortable rendezvous would be almost impossible. The prospect of rushing through 134 locks with the weather being as hot as it was, held little appeal. I was very relieved therefore, when Antoinette agreed to give up the whole idea. Having made that decision, we ended up staying for three nights in Charleville-Mézières to give ourselves ample time to explore the town.

It was only a short walk from the pleasure boat port to the imposing focal point of the town—the Place Ducale, overseen by a statue of Charles de Gonzague who founded the town in the seventeenth century. Twenty-three houses of faded red brick, with high, sloping, black slate roofs in the Louis XIII style, and linked together with symmetrical brick arches, enclose the square. Beneath the arches, one can wander in comfort away from the relentless heat of the summer sun, perusing at leisure the various shops that nestle beneath the brick canopy.

Away from the Place Ducale are shops and restaurants of every description. From a gardening shop, Antoinette purchased a pair of heavy duty gloves to protect her hands while handling the fore deck lines. By now, the daily handling of ropes and mooring lines was beginning to take its toll on hands that were more used to playing the delicate mechanism of a flute.

That night we strolled down the Rue Thiers République, avidly reading the menus displayed outside the many restaurants that flanked either side of the street. It was a tough decision, but we eventually seated ourselves at an outside table of a restaurant where we had previously cast an appreciative eye over the diners' plates, on our way past. It turned out to be a good choice and the meal lived up to our expectations. The additional bonus was being able to watch the large passing parade of other expectant diners who also strolled along the street reading every menu in sight.

We were quickly learning that, in France, the waiters expect you to have made your meal choice before actually being seated at the table. To the French, dining out is a very important business and they consider it unthinkable that one would select a restaurant without having first examined every detail of the displayed menu. Once we were seated at the table, we were surprised at the alacrity with which the waiter was anxious to take the order and to get things underway. We subsequently grew accustomed to this practice, and when you think about it, the custom makes perfect sense.

Strolling back to the boat in the velvet softness of the night air, we held hands, and contentedly discussed our plans for another early morning start. Once again, we decided that it would be sensible to leave early in the morning, and then to stop travelling before the heat of the day became too oppressive.

With this in mind, we slipped out of Charleville-Mézières just before 8.30 a.m. and reached the tiny village of Mouzon by mid afternoon. There was just enough space for us to moor up astern of a smart cruiser with a dark green hull, and which was flying the American flag. The pristine white superstructure of the cruiser made us look positively shabby by comparison. Up until now, I had held the self inflated opinion that we were just about the smartest craft around!

We had previously arranged with my cousin for Mouzon to be another drop off point for our mail and we were happy to see that the Mouzon Post Office was immediately adjacent to the port. Since leaving Amsterdam, we had also been in touch with the firm that had supplied all the curtains for the boat. We were still missing the final two curtains for the main saloon doors, and had requested that they mail the curtains to Mouzon. After we were secured alongside, Antoinette checked with the post office to see if the mail had arrived, but she was disappointed to find that it had not.

Around 5.00 p.m. we noticed the couple from the American cruiser *The Slow Lane* were on the dockside chatting to the Port Captain who had come around to collect the nominal port dues. We strolled over and introduced ourselves. Bill and Carol, we learnt, were from Hawaii, and like us, they had recently purchased their cruiser in Holland for an indefinite period of cruising in both Holland and France. They had just come from the Canal des Ardennes and were heading north towards Belgium. Over drinks, on board *The Slow Lane*, we exchanged stories of our cruising experiences so far.

The next evening we invited them aboard the *Bermuda II* for drinks, and Bill presented us with what looked like a packet of vacuum packed ball bearings. The silver coloured packet, we were surprised to discover, contained macadamia nuts from Hawaii. It turned out that Bill had a business interest in a firm that produced these luxury nuts for which Hawaii is famous. We also discovered that Carol was an electrical engineer by profession. They were an interesting couple and we wished that they had been heading south like us, which would have given us the opportunity to get to know them better.

The next day *The Slow Lane* left Mouzon, and I was still very envious of their bright white painted coachroof so I decided to paint ours, while we were waiting for the mail to arrive. A taxi ride from Mouzon to Berry-au-Bac, at the junction of the River Meuse and the Canal des Ardennes, resulted in the purchase of some white gloss paint, brushes, solvent and a few much needed extra fenders. The small chandlery store at Berry-Au-Bac catered more for small cruisers than boats the size of *Bermuda II* but small fenders were infinitely better than none at all.

Returning to the boat, we were just in time to assist the *Funny Girl*, a large yawl, with its masts stowed horizontally on deck, to tie up alongside us. Our new found berth mates had enthralling stories to tell about cruising in the Mediterranean where they had been for the past two years. The skipper, Erling Andreasen, had built the steel hulled boat himself and was taking the boat back to Denmark where he hoped to sell her and then to build another boat. The boat was in a very sad state. Piles of rusty anchor chain, and dilapidated gear were strewn all over the decks in a haphazard manner, giving a brief inkling as to the skipper's 'daredevil' attitude to life.

Erling told us that at the first lock, between the River Saône and the Canal de l'Est, the depth of the boat's keel had prevented him from floating over the concrete lock cill. He had promptly returned to a place called St. Jean-de-Losne and had one metre of keel cut off and sold for scrap. He proudly showed us the invoice and credit slip for the completed work and for the sale of the scrap lead and steel. He told us that he had been assured of a three day operation but it had subsequently taken three weeks. 'Beware the pirates of St. Jean-de-Losne,' he confided over a cold beer in the stifling heat of the boat's interior.

I vaguely remembered that this was the same place that Dick Hunt, whom we had met in Liège, had recommended as a good place to seek assistance if we had any engine problems on our way south. 'Two conflicting points of view,' I thought, as I mentally passed the information off. St. Jean-de-Losne lay on our route south and apart from an overnight stay, we probably would not see much of the place.

Erling showed us his diary which was a beautiful hand written, and illustrated account of his extended Mediterranean cruising. We were especially impressed by the pen and ink drawings which were done with considerable artistic talent. In the heat of the saloon, I looked forward to the prospect of the *Bermuda II* cruising on the sunlit dappled waters of the Mediterranean.

I was less pleased with Erling the next day however, when I discovered that he had walked over my freshly painted coachroof, which was still wet, when he returned to his boat in the early hours of the morning. The damage was done however, and there was no point in making a fuss about it.

The mail arrived on Wednesday, and the curtains arrived from Holland on Thursday, so we prepared ourselves for an early departure on Friday. After checking through the mail I was angry with the bank, in England, for not having sent an additional supply of Eurocheques, as they had promised. The credit cards that should have been dispatched many weeks earlier had also not been sent, as promised. We were not quite penniless, as I had some American dollars in cash that we always carried on board in case of an emergency, but if something did not happen soon, I could see difficulties on the horizon.

As a precaution, I telephoned the bank and made arrangements for them to transfer telegraphically some funds to the Banque Crédit Mutuale, in Verdun, where we expected to be in a few days. The voice on the other end of the telephone assured me that this would be done as soon as possible. After expressing my disgust at their track record so far, I hung up and returned to the boat where I continued to rub down Erling's footprints with sandpaper.

Later in the afternoon, Antoinette went into town in search of some steak for dinner. At the only butcher's shop in the main street, she discovered that the only meat available was horse steak, which she rapidly declined and beat a hasty retreat from the shop. To this day, we have still not experienced the French passion for horse meat although in later years, friends said that they would invite us over when they were cooking some, so that we could have a taste. Much to Antoinette's relief, and my sorrow, this never took place. Our planned early departure from Mouzon, was thwarted by Erling and his crew member who had both left the boat early in the morning, and had disappeared into town. To disappear in Mouzon is quite a trick as there is only one street and two bars, but they were nowhere to be seen. I could not simply shove their boat off and leave it to drift in the canal. At the same time, I knew that because of the remaining draught of the *Funny Girl*, I could not secure her alongside in our place. Erling eventually returned at 11.30 a.m. full of apologies and hurriedly cast off and continued his journey northwards.

Again there was no point in making a fuss, and truthfully the delay was of no consequence to us, but the wisdom of allowing other boats to moor alongside without agreeing to an exact departure time, was something that we would consider in the future. 'Perhaps Bill and Carol had been right when they had named their boat *The Slow Lane*,' I reflected later. This surely was the slow lane, and we would get to wherever it was that we were going, when we got there. *Quo Fata Ferunt*, I thought philosophically, bearing in mind the Latin motto painted on our bow.

The 'wherever' turned out to be the small town of Stenay whose centrally located pleasure port and peaceful surroundings beckoned us in with the promise of a tranquil overnight stay.

Antoinette consulted the *Michelin Guide*, and she was surprised to see that the small town boasted not one, but two, recommended restaurants. We decided to try the Auberge des Tilleuls on the Rue Jeanne d'Arc, which was only a short walk from the mooring. Antoinette enjoyed a delicately steamed turbot, and I had the Filet de

Canard. Both dishes were expertly prepared, and presented with eye catching appeal. The steamed vegetable platter was especially appreciated by Antoinette. My only complaint was that I found 60 French francs (which at the current rate of exchange came to £6) for two rather ordinary, and small, *Melon au Porto*, to be overpriced for what they were. The total bill, which included a rather unpretentious bottle of white wine, came to 426 French francs (£42.60). Given the opportunity, I would certainly dine there again, but I would be a little bit more cautious in my choice of hors-d'oeuvre, and I would probably query the 24 francs charged for a shot of inferior Cognac.

After a peaceful, undisturbed night, we were on our way by 10.00 a.m. on Saturday morning. We had visited the local bakery for some fresh baked croissants which were washed down with ample quantities of hot, freshly brewed, *café au lait*.

We passed through undulating countryside with fields of freshly mown hay whose unmistakable sweet aroma hung heavily in the summer air. We were now only a short distance away from the legendary town of Verdun, whose very name conjures up visions of the holocaust that was World War One.

At Lock 25 (Planchette), we met a very accommodating lock keeper. He was an elderly gentleman and his eyes sparkled with the wisdom of a long life. When we told him that we were looking for a place to stop for a couple of hours and to rest out of the heat of the sun, he graciously assisted us in mooring the boat under the only large tree on the landscape. The tree was located about 100 metres beyond the lock and the lock keeper assured us that we were welcome to spend the night there, if we wished.

The old man well remembered the horrors of the wars that had ravaged this area of France, and he seemed intent on recognizing the efforts of the Allies, by affording a warm welcome to any English speaking people that passed through his lock. We subsequently heard from other boaters that this charming gentleman was always the same, extending courtesy and the hand of friendship to all who passed by.

We thanked him in the best way we could, by giving him a selection of Bermuda souvenirs that we had purchased in Bermuda prior to our departure. From our past experiences of cruising France in hire boats, we knew that little items such as key rings, small penknives and badges were well received by the lock keepers and their children, but once again, our limited knowledge of French was proving to be a considerable handicap. After a two hour rest, we continued on our way to Consenvoye and we were soon moored in the very shallow, and very narrow, pleasure port. The surface of the water in the port was covered in water lilies, and I could see that the only way out in the morning would be to reverse slowly back through the narrow opening through which we had entered.

It was Sunday August 12th, when we eventually arrived in Verdun and moored alongside one of the convenient pontoons in the centre of the town. Today was our son's birthday. He was surprised, and pleased to receive our telephone call congratulating him on having reached the ripe old age of twenty-two. We could only talk for a short time as the units remaining on the telephone card were descending at an alarming rate on this long distance call to Bermuda.

We learnt that all was well with him, and with the rest of the family back in Bermuda.

'This is the life,' we had assured him. 'Not a care in the world; good food, good wine, interesting places to visit and friendly people.'

Little did we know, or suspect, the frustrating banking saga that was shortly to unfold before us.

Chapter 6

VERDUN

August 13th/18th, 1990

The very mention of the name Verdun, brings to mind images of World War I, when hundreds and thousands of soldiers died fighting for their country and their respective beliefs. In World War II, Verdun was also the scene of fierce fighting, and today, the countryside around Verdun is ringed with no less than seventy-four military cemeteries. The Douamont Ossuary alone contains the remains of 130,000 unknown soldiers, and in the adjacent national cemetery are the remains of 15,000 identified French soldiers. The remains of the old fortifications and the many monuments, together with the cemeteries, are a constant reminder of man's inhumanity to one another during times of war.

It is impossible to escape from the notorious past of the town, and even our splendid canalside mooring, was almost in the shadow of a famous monument—the imposing Victory Monument, inaugurated on 23rd June 1929, and backing on to the old twelfth-century ramparts was less than a minute away.

Shortly after our arrival we set about locating the Banque Crédit Mutuale that would hopefully yield some much needed cash. After a short walk, we were greeted by the sight of the familiar red and blue Crédit Mutuale logo, but the bank itself was closed. We had not been in France long enough yet to get used to the fact that most provincial banks are closed on Mondays.

On Tuesday, the bank was open and we inquired about our expected funds. After shuffling through a sheaf of papers, the manager told us that no funds for us had arrived yet. He also politely informed us that the next day was a public holiday and that I should therefore return on Thursday afternoon. Resigning ourselves to a two day wait, we explored the town and did some minor maintenance on the boat.

During the brief rain showers that we had encountered over the past week, the middle cabin had developed an annoying little leak that was right over the top bunk in the middle cabin. After a close inspection of the teak deck directly above the origin of the drip, I could see that the rubber deck sealant had pulled away from the metal underlay of the aft deck. Verdun is far inland from any nautical supplies and the only product that I could find in the local hardware shop was a black compound used for sealing around chimney bricks. After the first passing rain shower, at the conclusion of my repair efforts, I was pleased to see that the tell tale puddle did not appear on the plastic garbage bag that we had placed over the bunk mattress in order to protect it. I continued to prod and poke at the black compound for several weeks, but it was several months before the stuff eventually set up!

A noisy motor cycle disturbed our sleep that night, by roaring up and down the main road alongside the moorings. The rider had his racing track well defined, and by using the two bridges at either end of the mooring basin he had a perfect circuit.

After a fitful night's sleep I was not in the best of humour when I confronted the bank manager on Thursday morning. My humour darkened further when the manager apologetically informed me that he had still not received any advice regarding the money that we were expecting. In complete frustration, I telephoned the bank in England who confirmed that the money had been sent five days before. The bank agreed to start tracing the telegraphic transfer advice from their end.

Resuming our sightseeing of Verdun, we stumbled across, more by accident than design, the Musée de la Princerie. This small museum is located on the Rue de la Belle-Vièrge, and is contained in a Renaissance house that was built by a local churchman. The museum contains a comprehensive collection of interesting artifacts from the Bronze Age and Romano–Gallic period, and also displays a fine collection of Alsace-Lorraine ceramics and porcelain. Several rooms display seventeenth-century furniture in a remarkably well-preserved condition. There is so much of interest in this small museum that it is well worth a whole day's investigation.

After our visit to the museum we returned to the quayside, and saw that we had been joined by the *Atlantis* which was flying the New Zealand flag. This eye catching, Dutch built, cruiser was owned by Barry and Nancy Staite. They introduced themselves and their 6-year-old son George, and they invited us to join them after dinner, for coffee and drinks.

One thing that had concerned us when we had started to plan our two year cruise, was that our nomadic way of life would preclude us from striking up relationships with other people. This was proving to be far from reality. Already the social side of our lives was blossoming every day.

We went on board the *Atlantis* after dinner, and were introduced to the rest of the 'crew'. Neil and Justine, who were visiting from England, and Barry and Nancy's two year old daughter Catherine. Barry's sense of humour, and easy going manner, together with Nancy's down-to-earth and practical approach to life, made them a delightful couple. After half an hour, we felt like we had known them all our lives. Like us, they too, had decided to take two years off and investigate the inland waterways of Europe. They were at the end of their two year cruise and were returning to Holland where the *Atlantis* would be put up for sale.

The next evening, we returned their hospitality and invited them all on board the *Bermuda II* to continue the interesting conversation of the previous evening. As with Dick Hunt, in Liège, we were anxious to glean as much information about life on the canals as we possibly could.

Barry told us about the large sloping sided locks on the River Yonne, much feared by pleasure boaters with twin screwed craft. Although he claimed that he had still not figured out the best way to pass through a Yonne lock, he passed on a few tips that I mentally filed away for future use.

We found that we had much in common, and we were dismayed to hear that they planned to leave Verdun on Saturday and to continue on their way north. It was well after 1.00 a.m. when we finally turned in for the night.

Young George visited the boat early on Friday morning and proudly presented Antoinette with his latest work of art. It was a brightly coloured, felt tip drawing entitled 'My Garden—Love from George'. We were impressed with his art work, and his handwriting, which was advanced for a child of his age and reflected on Nancy's patient daily tuition. He also asked some pertinent questions like, 'How many litres of water does your washing machine use?' Sheepishly, I had to admit to not knowing the answer and promised myself a good bedtime read of the operating manual sometime.

After George had returned to the *Atlantis* I walked along the familiar streets, to the bank. Once again, I was told that no funds had been sent from England. Alarmed and annoyed, I went to the nearest telephone box and called the bank in England. Such was the extent of the verbal abuse that I poured out to the bank official, that I would not have been surprised to see smoke coming from the telephone wires. In no uncertain terms, he received what is commonly called, an earful. After threatening to return to England on the next available plane—something that would have been totally out of the question, I slammed the receiver back into place and stormed back to the boat. Antoinette has a much calmer nature than I, and she soothingly suggested that I return to the bank one last time.

With a determined look on my face and like a desperado about to commit a bank robbery, I burst through the swinging glass doors of the bank. I was greeted by a smiling bank manager, to whom my not so cheerful face had become well known over the past few days. He waved a piece of paper under my nose as if it were a treaty heralding a cessation of hostilities, and assured me that all was in order. The much sought after telegraphic transfer advice had finally arrived. Tapping the side of his nose solicitously, with the rolled up paper, he inquired as to how I would like the money. Somewhat unfairly, I told him that it made no difference to me, just so long as it bore some resemblance to French currency!

Returning to the boat, I gleefully fanned the money and suggested to Antoinette that we celebrate by having dinner in a nearby restaurant. As always, when dinner out is suggested, I did not have to repeat myself! A night out of the galley was always welcomed and we ended up dining in a restaurant, unimaginatively named The London Club. The food was very good, and my frustrations of the previous few days rapidly dissipated over a carafe of vin rosé.

On Saturday morning, we watched glumly as the *Atlantis* pulled away from the dock, and took up a position alongside us while we exchanged promises with Barry and Nancy to stay in touch.

'Not much of a day, Barry,' I said, looking at the overcast sky that threatened rain.

'No, you're right. But we really do have to get going.'

'If you stay, we could all go out for dinner and enjoy some of those excellent escargot at The London Club,' I tempted.

'No. Neil and Justine only have a short time off from work.'

'Well, no crew is going to thank you when it pours with rain, and you're lock bashing all day.' A flicker of indecision crossed his face as he glanced towards the heavens.

'Those escargot were some of the best I have ever had,' I said, pressing home the point. Once again he glanced heavenwards contemplating the gathering clouds. This time he shrugged his shoulders and smiled.

'You're right,' he said, as he put the boat into slow astern.

'What difference is one more day going to make?' he rationalized, as I took the mooring lines to secure the boat back into the berth that moments before they had just vacated.

'What time shall we all go for dinner then?' he asked

'7.30. OK?'

'Right, mate. We'll be ready then!'

We had a delightful meal. The conversation flowed just as easily as the wine. Antoinette was fascinated to find out that Neil who is a biologist by profession, was once a member of the punk culture, and at that time sported black leather, metal chains and a spiky hairstyle. It was rather difficult to believe that this well-spoken and casually dressed young man, who looked every inch the business professional, had ever adorned himself with black studded leather and purple hair. He told us that when he was 17, he had enjoyed the feeling of power as he entered a supermarket, or any other crowded establishment, dressed in his punk 'gear'. He relished the sense of power when people parted from his pathway like the Red Sea before Moses. We laughed at his tales, and shook our heads, still not quite believing that he had once been such a renegade.

Barry, Nancy and Justine, took it in turns to slip out of the restaurant frequently to check that the small children were safely asleep on board the *Atlantis* which was moored across the street from the restaurant. After a very late night, and a most enjoyable evening, we finally returned to our respective boats.

Chapter 7

Verdun to Toul
87.6 kilometres, 30 locks

August 19th/22nd, 1990

We did not make the early start that we had planned for in departing Verdun. Perhaps the farewell dinner, and the copious amounts of wine the previous night had something to do with it, but in any event a 10.00 a.m. start seemed fair and reasonable under the circumstances.

It was a pleasantly warm day, but it was not the searing heat that we had experienced prior to our arrival in Verdun. We took our time to amble along, at peace with the world. The scenery was not very interesting and consisted mainly of rolling pasture land on both sides of the canal. As there was not many locks on this section of the canal, it was not long before Antoinette disappeared below to the galley, and a short time later, mouth watering aromas came wafting up from below. 'My, my,' I thought, 'We really are getting settled into this way of life.' Up until now Antoinette was always on deck when we were underway. Our daily cruising had been so interesting that she could not bear to miss out on one inch of the passing countryside. Judging from the aromas that were reaching my steering position on the aft deck, a beef stew was being prepared in the galley, and I guessed that it would be ready for the table once we had stopped for the night.

At our last lock of the day, Lock 11 (Rouvrois) the lock keeper was kind enough to warn us that there was an oncoming barge expected, and that we would meet it in the next section.

Panic stations! I dispatched Antoinette to the bow to listen carefully while we were underway, and to see if she could detect the sound of the approaching barge's engine. We were travelling through a very winding, and twisting section of the canal, which meant that we could not see much more than a couple of hundred metres ahead of us. I approached each bend cautiously, with my heart hammering in my chest. This section of the canal was also just as narrow as the section where *Bermuda II* had received a tremendous smack on the port side transom, a week or so earlier.

'I can hear it!' shouted Antoinette from her vantage position at the bow. I jumped involuntarily in anticipation, and throttled back to an even slower pace than which we had been travelling.

The 'killer machine' swept around the next corner laden almost to the gunnels. The two large black anchors looked like malevolent black eyes against the grey painted hull. I could tell from the sound of the barge's engine that the skipper had reduced his forward speed. As the bow wave of the barge slowly subsided, 350 tonnes of pugnacious waterway might lined itself up with our bow and 23 tons of my precious boat!

Back in Verdun, Barry had taught us the art of passing barges in the narrow canal sections. He had taught us the theory at least, and now I was about to put the theory into practice. 'Hope you're right mate,' I muttered under my breath. 'Or else there's going to be one hell of a "clang" any minute.'

Lined up bow to bow, and dead centre of the canal, the *Bermuda II* and the barge converged on each other. Ten metres from certain impact, I flicked the bow of *Bermuda II* over to starboard. The barge did not exactly 'flick' its bow, but moved slowly, like a ponderous grey whale, over to starboard also. As we drew amidships of each other we both moved our wheels to port. This had the effect of moving the barge's stern safely over, and out of the way, allowing us to nip into the centre of the canal in its wake.

We had done it! We had safely passed a 'killer machine' in a very narrow waterway. I said a few silent words of thanks to Barry, 'Saint' springing irreverently to mind. Antoinette came aft and gave me a big hug.

'You did it! Well done,' she said.

'Yes, but if it had not been for Barry it might well have ended up being a different story,' I replied.

I had now learnt one of the basic manoeuvres of canal cruising. Over the next two years, we never had another problem when passing barges. Although we were both experienced sailors, our knowledge of inland navigation had been confined to hire boat holidays on the Canal du Midi and the Brittany canals, where very little commercial traffic had existed. In fact, commercial traffic on the Brittany canals ended sometime in the 1970s and on the Midi it finished entirely in 1989. Most hire boats were half the beam of the *Bermuda II*, and inland cruising is a far cry from the open water sailing which we had been used to.

At 5.00 p.m. we arrived at St Mihiel. We were surprised to find that the municipal council of this small village, had placed pontoons with water and electricity points, conveniently close to the bridge over which the main road passes on its way into the village. It was a very pleasant mooring. The river was wide and an ancient red-tiled, and wooden timbered, wash house on the opposite bank was festooned with red geraniums and added to the charisma of the place.

We were even more surprised when we read the notice board on shore. It informed us that we were welcome to stay here for up to forty-eight hours, and unlike other municipal moorings we had visited, water and electricity were free of charge. We immediately decided to stay the full permitted forty-eight hours.

The next morning, we found a good supermarket just a short distance from the mooring, and stocked up on essential supplies. We also purchased some other items from the small village shops, so in our own little way we did something in return for their hospitable mooring site. The rest of the day was taken up by doing all those necessary chores that have to be done frequently when living on a boat. Raw water filters had to be checked, batteries, bilges and shower pump filters were all becoming part of our daily lives. Antoinette completed her daily, and never ending, cleaning routine and settled down to a session of letter writing and updating her meticulous daily journal which she had kept faithfully since our departure from Bermuda.

Toul is only fifty-three kilometres away from St. Mihiel and given an early morning start, it would probably be possible to cover the distance in one day, but we decided to take our time and to spend the Tuesday night forty-three kilometres further down the canal, in the small village of Plagny. We found good complimentary mooring pontoons here also, but without water and electricity. Apart from the village baker, we found no other shops or restaurants in the immediate area.

47

Before we reached Toul on Wednesday, we had to go through the 500-metre-long Foug tunnel. The entrance to the tunnel is controlled by a traffic light system and the tunnel presented us with no problems.

On the outskirts of Toul we were met by a travelling lock keeper who rode ahead of us in his car, and operated the locks that led to the town centre. The lock keeper's son and a friend, who were both about 12 years old, were on their summer holidays, and they were delighted to accept our invitation to travel on the boat with us. Father, having lost what I suspect were his two assistants, did all the work at each lock. As all the locks were mechanized, this only involved button pushing to operate the lock machinery.

The two boys chatted away in French. Once again, our limited knowledge of the language was a drawback. Armed with a copy of the French/English dictionary, we heard all about 'Jacko' the pet crow who hated the rain and who would seek shelter in the house whenever it rained. At least, I think that was the story! Both of the boys were a delight to have on board and they punctuated their stories with comical gesticulations just to make sure that we had some idea as to what they were talking about. At the last lock before Toul, Antoinette brought out a large tin of 'Quality Street' chocolates and invited them to each take a handful before they clambered ashore and re-joined the lock keeper. Their hands promptly grew to a good size twelve, and half a tin of 'Quality Street' found its way ashore.

In bright sunshine we eventually entered the large port basin of Toul. The Port de Plaisance was bedecked with flags and a large fountain placed in the centre of the harbour, cascaded jets of sparkling water into the air. Colourful flower beds dotted the surrounding grass lawns and enhanced the appearance of this busy mooring basin.

We had no trouble finding a vacant berth alongside the main wall of the port, and after securing the boat we sat in the saloon, out of the heat of the afternoon sun, and debated our next move. We were thinking about taking the boat up the ten kilometre embranchment canal to Nancy, a city that we were very interested in visiting because of its well known, and excellent museums. It was not to be long however, before we were advised against doing this, by two gentlemen who were very knowledgeable about such matters.

Chapter 8

TOUL

August 23rd/26th, 1990

It was going to be a very hot day. The early morning sun shone down on the pleasure boat moorings of Toul from a cloudless sky. Not a wisp of wind disturbed the flags of many nations that flew from the stern of each boat according to its origin. The ducks floated like unblinking wooden decoys on the still waters of the mooring basin.

We decided that we would walk into the main shopping district, before the streets became uncomfortably hot. We left a couple of films for developing at a camera shop that advertised a forty-eight hour developing service, and then investigated the many shops in the area. We really did not need anything so our shopping was more idle curiosity than a determined foraging expedition. We did purchase a bottle of Scotch and several bottles of wine for the liquor locker but it was more by impulse than by design. On the way back to the boat we stopped at a small grocery store and stocked up on fresh fruit and vegetables. The owner was a jovial fellow of Cypriot origin who spoke English and who took considerable pride in showing off his linguistic abilities to his French speaking clientele. Because of his outgoing manner and cheerful sales patter, we probably ended up buying slightly more than we had intended, but the quality of the produce was superb.

After a light luncheon of freshly sliced baguette filled with cold meats and salad, followed by some juicy ripe plums, we were contemplating taking an afternoon siesta when there was a knock on the saloon door that faced the quay.

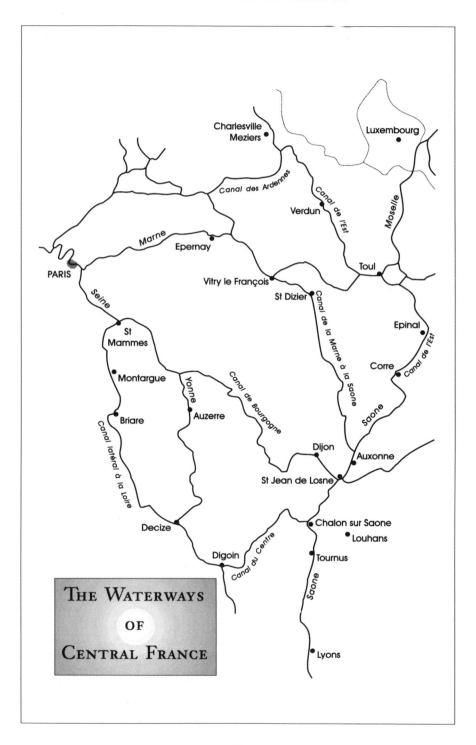

THE WATERWAYS OF CENTRAL FRANCE

Two smartly dressed customs officers, complete with side arms, as is the fashion in France, stood on the quayside.

'*Bonjour, monsieur.* We are from the customs department and we would like to come aboard and inspect your boat and the ships papers.' I had heard, and read about some extraordinary stories of French bureaucracy and I was anxious to get off on the right foot.

'Come aboard, gentlemen, and please sit down,' I said. Once seated I asked them if they would like a drink as it was very hot outside and they were both perspiring heavily. They both nodded in agreement.

'A little chilled rosé wine?' I asked.

'*Non, merci.*'

'A cold beer perhaps?'

'*Non, merci.*'

Thinking that by offering alcohol I might be committing some cardinal sin, I was about to suggest tea or coffee when I noticed them eyeing the bottle of Scotch that we had just purchased in town. It was still sitting prominently on top of the drinks cupboard.

'A little whisky then?' I said hopefully.

'*Oui, merci,*' they replied in unison. Once I had poured a good shot of whisky into each of the two glasses, I could see that they were now ready to get down to business.

Unfastening a leather brief case, one of the officers produced a sheaf of paper and requested our passports, the ship's passport, the insurance documents, the VHF radio licence and proof of my ability to be in charge of the vessel. Nervously, I watched as they checked each document and meticulously transcribed the details to one of the many forms that had been produced from the briefcase. This took quite some time—long enough for the whisky glasses to be charged twice more before they had recorded all the details. We had truthfully answered all the questions about where we were going, where we had come from, our intended length of stay and dozens of questions that seemed to be totally unrelated to our present circumstances. The answers to the questions were dutifully recorded on the continuous supply of forms that kept on appearing from the depths of the briefcase.

As the afternoon wore on, the contents of the whisky bottle slowly diminished. Inversely, the atmosphere became more friendly and more relaxed, so much so, that I finally asked why it was necessary to obtain all the details that they were gathering for supposedly customs purposes.

'Oh, but *monsieur Capitaine*, we finished with the customs details ages ago. We are now gathering information for a survey by the Chamber of Commerce in Nancy!' I was very relieved to hear this, and I no longer felt like an escapee from a top security prison that was owned and operated by the government of the Fifth Republic.

The two officers had by this time been on our boat for two hours, and with the whisky acting as a lubricant to their tongues, they were only too willing to answer our questions about their jobs in the customs service.

'This morning we had some good luck. We intercepted a load of cocaine that was being smuggled into France by road,' they confided.

'*Une bonne-affaire*! But as soon as we came on your boat, I could tell that you were not cocaine,' said the younger of the two, waving an extended forefinger in the air for added emphasis. 'We have sniffer dogs, too!'

This last piece of information came as a nasty surprise. The very thought of a large and agressive 'Fido' chomping his way through the mahogany lockers was not a pleasant one, and although we were completely innocent, I quickly changed the subject and told them of our plans to take the boat up the branch canal to Nancy.

'This you must not do. Close to the boat moorings in Nancy there are many gypsies and should you leave your boat unattended, *pouf—* everything will be stolen.' Visions of a swarthy, bandanna clad individual carrying the ship's wheel down the back streets of Nancy immediately sprang to mind. They went on to relate many tales of woe regarding pleasure boats that had moored in Nancy. We decided right then, that we would leave the boat in Toul and visit Nancy by train. This met with their unanimous approval and at 4.30 p.m. somewhat the worse for wear, they cheerfully wished us '*Bon voyage*' and staggered off in the direction of the car park.

The next day we travelled by train to the city of Nancy, which took about twenty minutes in a blissfully air-conditioned carriage. We walked from the railway station to the Place Stanislas in the centre of the city, where we found the impressive Neptune fountain which was constructed between 1752 and 1756. A visit to the nearby tourist information office confirmed our feelings that there was a lot of interesting things to see in Nancy. It would be impossible to see everything in just one day, so we confined ourselves to a visit to Le

Musée des Beaux-Arts where an impressive collection of paintings by such famous artists as Monet, Manet, Utrillo, Lautrec and Rubens were complemented by an interesting display of Daum glassware.

At the end of the afternoon, tired and footsore we took the train back to Toul. The train was full of young army conscripts and the standing room only ride did nothing to ease our aching feet. We treated ourselves to an excellent early dinner at the restaurant La Belle Epoque which is on the Avenue Victor Hugo, conveniently situated within sight of the boat mooring basin.

The next day, while we were doing the daily clean up routine of the boat, we had the pleasure of meeting Richard, an American who lives in Toul. He stopped by the boat to introduce himself and to inquire if there was anything that he could do for us. Upon learning that I had been searching for an oil syphon, Richard very kindly offered to drive me to the Le Clerc supermarket on the outskirts of Toul. He was sure that I would find what I was looking for in the automotive department. He was exactly right and I found the syphon that I had been looking for. When we had returned to the boat I extended an invitation to both Richard and his wife to join us on board for drinks, later that evening, in order to thank him for his kindness.

Sitting in the saloon that evening, Richard told us that he was stationed in France with the U.S. forces during World War Two and that after the war he returned to France to marry his wartime sweetheart. We were also delighted to hear about the ancient history of Toul as a military stronghold and the fact that this tradition is continued today as on the outskirts of the town there is a significant military base.

The following day, Richard paid us one last visit and brought with him a gift of Mirabelle plums from his own garden, and for which the region is well known. After making sure that everything was fine with us, he bade us farewell and wished us good luck on our journey south.

Chapter 9

Toul to Fontenoy-Le-Château
125.6 kilometres, 81 locks

August 27th/September 1st, 1990

Heavy fog prevented us from leaving the pleasure boat basin in Toul until late morning, but we made good use of the time while waiting for the fog to lift. I walked to the post office to mail the many letters that we had both written in the past five days, and Antoinette ran one last load of washing through the machine before we finally got underway.

Due to a series of heavy delays, that were a result of having to wait for commercial traffic at each of the locks that we passed through, we progressed only a few kilometres before deciding in the late afternoon, to stop for the night. We found a suitable wild mooring about 500 metres downstream from Lock 41 (Crevechamps). Once we had secured the boat alongside the corrugated steel sheeting that lined both banks of the canal, and had taken care of Antoinette's encounter with some stinging nettles while jumping ashore to secure the bow line, we walked down to the lock and asked the lock keeper for permission to moor in that position for the night. He assured us that it was quite all right as we were far enough away from the lock not to cause any obstruction, and wished us a pleasant evening. We were way out in the countryside. Fields of cattle corn stretched into the distance as far as the eye could see. Before dinner we walked a short distance along the rudimentary towpath before clumps of brambles prevented us from going any further. We were completely alone and we were very happy to be in our own little world of peace and quiet.

After a simple meal, we retired to our bunks to read, but not before I had checked and tightened the mooring lines outside in the pitch black night.

At 6.45 a.m. the next day, we were suddenly awakened by the sound of the mooring lines creaking and gently straining against the boat's bollards. We were still new at canal cruising but we both knew that this meant that either a lock keeper had emptied his lock upstream, or something was coming. I pulled on my jeans and threw a sweater over my T-shirt and went up to the saloon and looked out. The *Bermuda II* was enveloped in a fog so thick that I could barely see our bow just ten metres from where I stood.

I moved down to the galley and put the morning coffee on to perk and then returned to the saloon and stood silently in the open door-way. A few moments later I was horrified to see a huge black wall of steel slide slowly past, only one metre away from the open starboard side door. An unladen 38 metre *péniche* was silently moving past in conditions that I considered to be totally unsafe. From his wheelhouse, it was not possible for the skipper of the barge to see his bow, let alone any oncoming boats. We could only presume that he had been in radio contact with the Crevechamps lock keeper who must have advised him of our mooring spot. I can appreciate that time means money to barge captains but in my opinion, this was a foolhardy, and dangerous way to navigate. The barge slowly disappeared, swallowed up in the swirling fog.

The fog lifted by mid morning, having been burnt off by a searing morning sun, allowing us to cover the twenty kilometres and eleven locks to Charmes, without incident. By mid afternoon we were comfortably tied up at a mooring within easy walking distance of the town centre.

It was not long after our arrival before we had attracted a crowd of young boys who had been swimming in the murky canal. They asked if it would be possible for them to dive off the aft deck of the boat and practise their diving skills. It seemed a harmless enough request, and so after making sure that the boat was secured and locked up, I drew aside the eldest boy. I told him that we were going shopping in the town and after laying down some ground rules, put him in charge of both the boat and the swimming party in our absence. He immediately took to his newly elevated position with considerable pride and promptly ticked off two of the younger members for diving off the teak rail and not the deck!

We walked leisurely around the town of Charmes before returning to the boat, and being met, quite excitedly, by our newly appointed *chef du bateau*. Growing three inches in height he told us that some customs officers had visited the boat while we were away. Proudly, he had told the customs officers that he was in charge of the boat, and that the owners were not expected to return for quite some time. Apparently satisfied, the customs officers had declined to wait, and had departed, thus in all likelihood saving us the trouble of going through another lengthy paperwork exercise, as we had done a week earlier in Toul. My replacement bottle of whisky would probably last a bit longer, too!

We were able to get underway from Charmes the next morning at a reasonable hour, as there was no repeat of the fog that had caused us both alarm, and delay, on the previous morning. We were now on the southern branch of the Canal de l'Est and we noticed a marked change in both the lock keepers' attitude, and in the locks themselves. Most of the locks were in a dilapidated state of repair, and the lock keepers decidedly less friendly than their counterparts on the northern branch.

One exception to this observation was a brightly decorated and well kept lock in the care of a retired barge skipper. Outside the blue and yellow painted lock keeper's cottage, a stack of used rubber tyres, complete with ropes attached, were offered for sale as makeshift boat fenders. The use of rubber tyres for fenders is strictly frowned on by the French authorities, unless the tyre contains an inflated inner tube to keep it afloat if it is inadvertently dropped into the canal. The navigational guide book pointed out that each year many temporary stoppages are caused by rubber tyres falling into the water and jamming the lock gates and sluice mechanisms. Having by now blown out two of our four heavy duty fenders, we were only too pleased to purchase three of these illegal fenders, and to turn a blind eye to the regulations. Just in case we were to run foul of the law, I made sure that we had our photograph taken with the lock keeper and the offending tyres, hoping to claim innocence of the law if questioned.

At one lock, on the outskirts of Thaon les Vosges, a lady lock keeper, with all the aerodynamics of a sub post office, moved with such determined slowness, that I thought it would be mid winter before we got through the lock. I willingly assisted in closing the rear gates once the *Bermuda II* was secured in the lock, but she still had to operate the paddle mechanism with the winch handle which she jealously guarded. The whole process was done in a painfully slow and laboured manner.

We passed through another six locks and then took the small, weed infested and overgrown branch canal up to Épinal where we planned to stay for two nights.

The moorings at Épinal are directly opposite a huge warehouse or distribution centre where large articulated trucks were constantly loading or unloading day and night. This was not the place to find peace and quiet, but the town itself is pleasant enough and offers every imaginable shopping facility.

The next evening, two men from the navigation authority visited the boat and asked us when we would be leaving Épinal to tackle the flight of fourteen locks at Golbey. This was to be our first experience of continuous locking and I had no idea as to the difficulties involved, or how long it would take. I told the two men that we would leave our moorings at 9.15 a.m. and would present ourselves at the first lock of the staircase by 9.30 a.m. This met with their approval and they wished us *au revoir* till the morning.

As bad luck would have it, the morning was cold and misty. A drizzling rain made us wish that we had stayed in the warmth of our beds. It took us three hours of intermittent motoring and mooring, before we were through the last lock of the Golbey flight.

We were now at the second highest summit level of any canal in France. The 10.8-kilometre-long *Bief de partage* is at an altitude of 360 metres (1,181 feet) above sea level, and is only surpassed by the 378.50 metre (1,242 feet) summit level of the Canal de Bourgogne.

After the last lock of the Golbey flight, we felt that we had done enough locking for the day, and therefore did not press on any further than Chaumousey where we found a silted up turning basin that allowed us just enough length, and depth, to moor the boat on the bow and stern anchor. At anchor in this fashion, we were well clear of the parallel navigation channel. One drawback was that we could not get off the boat as we still lacked the dinghy that I had been promising myself and which would eventually hang from the stern davits of *Bermuda II*.

At 7.15 a.m. the next day, a barge heading downstream appeared ghostlike out of the mist astern of us. Antoinette recorded the scene in what later turned out to be a spectacular photograph. The mist lifted quickly, and we were soon underway, following the barge downstream. From now on, it was all downhill to the Mediterranean and I could not imagine anything that would prevent us from enjoying the Mediterranean sun all winter long.

The descent from the summit level to the River Saône follows the Coney River valley and passes through some of the wildest and most beautiful countryside that we had seen to date with the exception of the Ardennes region in Belgium. Dense pine forests punctuated by tumbling, crystal clear streams cascading into the valley were a delight to the eye. On numerous occasions the canal was carried over small streams by aqueducts which gave us a bird's eye view of the rugged terrain beneath us.

Students at isolated locks, carrying out their summer jobs as lock keepers, were often surprised at our approach. One young lady, sun bathing, and caught in a considerable state of *déshabillé* was particularly startled as we made our slow approach to a lock surrounded on all sides by a wall of coniferous forest. Somewhat sheepishly, and with a blush that darkened her already bronzed features, she rapidly replaced her clothing and I was spared the tantalising prospect of a lock keeper carrying out her duties *au naturel*.

It was a very long day, and I was concerned that we would not arrive at Fontenoy-le-Château before the 7.30 p.m. lock closing time. I need not have worried. At the penultimate lock before Fontenoy-le-Château the lock keeper told us that he would ride along the towpath in his car and operate the last remaining lock to enable us to reach the mooring basin in Fontenoy. We therefore arrived at the mooring basin in Fontenoy at 7.45 p.m. after a day in which we had set a new personal record of negotiating thirty-five locks in one day. Our record was at the expense of yet another of our large fenders, the frequent abrasion against the rough stone sides of the locks causing its demise. We were pleased that we had purchased the rubber tyres from the

Alongside at Fontenoy-le-Château.

friendly lock keeper, two days previously, as they were now being pressed into service.

The mooring basin at Fontenoy is a very agreeable place to stay as it is shielded on the eastern side by large trees, which reduce the heat of the early morning summer sun, and on the western side by a steeply rising hillside. For a couple of hours either side of midday it was quite hot and airless, but once the sun dips behind the western hillside it becomes an ideal place to sit outside and dine alfresco on the deck.

The Crown Blue Line hire boat company has a base in the basin, and we made friends with an American group who had rented a boat for a two week period. They planned to cruise downstream, and to terminate their holiday at St. Jean-de-Losne, where there was another Blue Line base. We entertained them to drinks on the aft deck during which they offered to give us any left over grocery supplies from the hire boat, should we meet up with them in St. Jean-de-Losne.

'Only a slight chance of that,' I said. 'I think that we will be passing right through. If we do stop though, we'll be sure to look you up and find out how you enjoyed your cruising holiday.'

Moored alongside the quay in Fontenoy is the restaurant barge the

Deo Gratias, and it was here that we discovered one of the best values for money that we had ever come across. A sumptuous meal of *soupe de poisson*, veal, entrecote steak, dessert, cheese, Irish coffee and a bottle of Rosé de Provence came to just 305 francs (£30.50) and was presented and served with both style and elegance.

We thoroughly enjoyed this charismatic little town and we stayed four nights, after which we were well rested and ready to tackle the remaining twenty-two kilometres of the canal before it linked up with the River Saône at the town of Corre.

Chapter 10

Fontenoy-le-Château to St. Jean-de-Losne
186.1 kilometres, 31 locks

September 5th/11th, 1990

Before leaving Fontenoy-le-Château, it was necessary to fill up our water tanks. Under normal circumstances this would not be an event worthwhile recording, however, the water tap at Fontenoy is located some distance away from the canalside moorings. We discovered that the length of hose that we carried on board was not long enough, by a good five or six metres, to make the connection to the water tap. Two other skippers, one Dutch and one French, were also having the same problem.

Here we were, Bermudians in the middle of France with one Dutchman and one Frenchman. Neither of us spoke each other's language proficiently enough to carry on a reasonable conversation, but we had a common problem! Necessity being the mother of invention, we succeeded, through a mixture of sign language and good will, in connecting up our three hoses. Like our language, they were not fitted with compatible connectors. Using a collection of jubilee clips, adhesive tape and soft wire, we eventually filled up all three boats with fresh water, and congratulated ourselves with a universal handshake!

We arrived at Corre in the late afternoon, and had great difficulty in finding a suitable mooring. We could see that a new port was under construction, but it would be a few months yet before it was ready to receive its first customers.

A large bulldozer was parked almost on the very edge of the canal, and after checking both the front and rear end to see if the sprouting grass had recently been disturbed, I concluded that the machinery had been left idle for quite some time. We moored up alongside the bulldozer and used its large rear towing hook on which to secure one of our mooring lines. We laughed at our fantasy of a 23 ton boat being dragged down the road early the next morning should the owner return and decide to move the bulldozer while the occupants of the boat were still asleep!

We need not have worried, and we passed an uneventful night. Apart from a reasonably good supermarket, Corre seemed to have little else to offer, so after the usual stocking up of the ship's supplies, we left late in the day, and headed for Port sur Saône.

The port de plaisance at Port sur Saône is well kept and offers good overnight moorings and there is also a restaurant called the Châlet à la Plage located close by. We chose however, to walk the short distance into town and ended up dining in the restaurant La Marine where the staff were friendly and the food modestly priced.

The next day, passage through the 680-metre-long St. Aubin tunnel was incredibly easy in comparison to the low roofed Ham tunnel. This tunnel is well lit and has a high concrete roof.

Our overnight berth in the pleasure port in Seveux seemed peaceful enough despite a French family noisily celebrating, with friends, the purchase of a new cruiser, in the opposite berth. I was not happy to be woken up at 2.00 a.m. and to receive an intoxicated invitation to join them on their boat for a drink. My ungracious reply needed no translation into French!

The next morning we left as quietly as we possibly could, but I was sorely tempted to bang on their boat and to invite them on board the *Bermuda II* for an early morning cup of coffee. I thought better of it however, and left them to their slumbers.

We were about thirty metres into the 600-metre-long Savoyeux tunnel, when we noticed a bright white light seemingly stationary in the distance. I reversed slowly back out of the tunnel and it was quite some time before a laden barge, with a brightly lit searchlight and travelling at a snail's pace, finally exited from the tunnel into the daylight. We noticed that the traffic lights, at the entrance to the tunnel, which had previously shown neither green or red, were now operating and showed a welcome green light.

After passing through Lock 13 (Savoyeux) the river widened considerably, and it was possible to make a quick passage downstream to the town of Gray. The town had originally sprung up around a fortress above the river, and due to its strategic location, it was destroyed and rebuilt many times. After resisting the army of Louis XIV for three days and nights it was not until 1674 that the town of Gray was annexed to France.

We found a mooring downstream of the lock at Gray, conveniently close to the Intermarche supermarket, and just a short walk from the interesting shops that lined the pedestrian precinct. Due to the limited mooring facilities for pleasure boats, it was not long before other pleasure boats, spied the convenient bulk of the *Bermuda II* and moored up alongside our starboard side. Our American friends that we had met in Fontenoy-le-Château were the first alongside, quickly followed by a Danish sailboat on passage from the Mediterranean back to Denmark, and a small Dutch cruiser that was also heading north.

That night we had dinner in the restaurant Hôtel Bellevue situated on the Avenue Carnot which was just a short walk from the boat. The staff were very friendly, and for a total of 348 francs (£35.00) we had a good meal served in agreeable surroundings. The food was not, surprisingly, up to the standard of the *Deo Gratias* back in Fontenoy, but it was pleasant enough.

In between visiting the Notre Dame Basilica, which was built between 1480 and 1530, and which is a remarkable specimen of Gothic architecture, and between visiting the beautiful municipal gardens, we were content to just laze in the sun, write letters and investigate the shops nearby to the boat.

After three relaxing days in Gray, we decided that it was time to push on downriver towards the ever beckoning sea.

Since leaving Corre, we had been having intermittent problems with the starboard engine overheating. We remembered Dick Hunt's advice, given in Liège, and decided that we would stop *en route* at St. Jean-de-Losne to seek assistance. In Liège, we had not considered that we might run into any difficulties, but Antoinette had thoughtfully scribbled down the information on the appropriate page of the navigation guide. Dick had told us that there were two boat yards in St. Jean-de-Losne and he had given us the name of the boat yard and the proprietor's name of the establishment that he recommended.

We motored downstream, frequently starting and stopping the starboard engine while underway, hoping that if the problem was a blockage of some sort, it might clear itself. The engine continued to overheat so we stopped in the early afternoon at Auxonne having run most of the distance using only the port side engine.

As we made our approach to the mooring pontoon, a gentleman from another boat that was already moored alongside, stood ready to take our lines and to assist us in docking the boat. Once safely secured alongside, the gentleman turned his attention to our Bermuda flag that was flying from the stern.

'You're from Bermuda are you? he asked. I was quite taken aback for this was the first person that recognised our flag since leaving Holland in July. I glanced over to his boat the *Beulah IV* and could see that the boat was flying the Red Ensign.

'Yes. We are both from Bermuda. Do you have any connections there?'.

'Oh, I have visited there. My wife's sister-in-law lives there,' he said laconically.

We promised to stop by the *Beulah IV* once we had tidied up the boat and concluded all the necessary engine checks that we did at the end of each day's cruising.

Later that evening, we met Peter and Germaine Brotherton on board their boat, *Beulah IV*. We were surprised to learn that Germaine's brother had, at one time, been a chief justice in Bermuda. They seemed to be a rather shy, quiet couple, so after a brief conversation we did not want to intrude further and so we returned to the *Bermuda II*. Little did we know that this was the beginning of a delightful and enduring friendship.

The next day, we took time off from banging around in the engine room with hammers and wrenches as we contrived to take a large portion of the engine cooling system apart—all to no avail.

In the castle beside the River Saône, lies Auxonne's most important claim to fame as it was here between 1788 and 1791 that Napoléon Bonaparte served as a lieutenant before beginning his illustrious future. The remains of the castle and ramparts, built by Louis XI, can be visited but it was closed during our brief stay. Instead we visited the impressive church with its mass of gargoyles and statues. Six of the statues in the sixteenth-century porch are copies of the statues from

The Moses Fountain by Claus Sluter who worked from about 1380 to 1400 for the rich Dukes of Burgundy in Dijon.

It is only eighteen kilometres from Auxonne to St. Jean-de-Losne and only one lock had to be negotiated on this beautiful stretch of river. Again, we were in no hurry, and despite the nagging worry over the engine, we really enjoyed the pastoral scenery that unfolded around every bend of the river.

Shortly after 11.30 a.m. the town of St. Jean-de-Losne came into view. The church with its spire and Burgundian tiled roof stood prominently alongside the bridge which spanned the river. Quite a few barges were tied up here, and we learnt from our canal guide that St. Jean-de-Losne is considered to be a bargeman's town.

We slipped beneath the stone arch of the bridge which leads to the Gare d'eau, and observed a rather dilapidated wooden sign which indicated that the place we were looking for, H_2O lay directly ahead of us. We could see many pleasure boats of every description moored to the finger pontoons and in the far corner of the boat basin the Crown Blue Line hire boat base was a hive of activity.

'Well, if all else fails, Crown Blue Line must have a couple of mechanics. Maybe, we could get one of them to take a look,' I said to Antoinette.

'Let's get alongside first, and investigate after lunch,' she replied.

A tall, distinguished looking man, wearing a white singlet, shorts and a sun hat, stood on the end of one of the finger pontoons, moving his hands up and down vertically, as if inquiring as to our draught.

'One metre twenty-five,' I shouted in my best French.

'Oh, that's all right, plenty of water, come ahead,' he responded in English. It was obvious that I had failed my French oral exam once again! Moving the boat slowly into the indicated vacant berth, the gentleman took our ropes and secured us alongside.

'How long will you be staying?'

'Just a couple of nights. Just long enough to get an engine problem sorted out. I'm actually looking for a Monsieur Gérard,' I said hopefully.

'Oh, that's my son, Charles. I am Herman Gérard,' he said extending his hand. We shook hands and I introduced Antoinette who was still standing in the bow tidying up the fore deck lines.

'Everyone is at lunch now, but my son should be in the office after

65

lunch,' he said, indicating a rustic-looking structure a short distance away. We had been joined on the pontoon by another man clad in the traditional mechanics uniform of blue overalls.

'What seems to be the problem then?' he asked, in an accent with an unmistakable Canadian twang. I briefly explained the problem and in return learnt that his name was Jack and that he was temporarily employed by H_2O as a mechanic.

'I can take a look right now,' he said, clambering onto the boat. Surprised, but relieved by this prompt service, I invited him to share our rudimentary sandwich lunch first, as we had not yet eaten. He readily accepted, and settled down to a glass of wine, while Antoinette busied herself in the galley.

At 2.00 p.m. Jack was still chatting away—no further mention of the engine having been made. I excused myself from the conversation, and left him in the company of Antoinette, while I walked up to the office, intent on locating M. Charles Gérard.

I knocked, and then pushed open the office door and entered the interior. Two men who had previously been engaged in an animated conversation promptly fell silent on my entry.

'Good day, I am looking for Monsieur Charles Gérard,' I said in French.

'Well, you have found him,' said the taller of the two, in English. 'That's the second time today that I have failed my French exam,' I thought sadly. Unwinding himself from the chair like a Swiss army knife, M. Gérard stood up and towered over me as we shook hands.

'What can I do for you?' he asked softly, eyeing me up and down. Visions of the St. Jean-de-Losne pirates that Erling had warned us about in Mouzon, swam through my head as I explained the problem that we were having with the engine.

'No problem,' said M. Gérard. 'I will be down in a moment to take a look, but first I should like to present my business partner, M. Robert Bond.' I shook hands with the jovial looking M. Bond, as once again the 'pirate' vision danced before my eyes. Although M. Gérard had a sort of swashbuckling manner about him, Erling's pirates clearly did not live here. As M. Gérard prepared to don a pair of one time white overalls, I retreated to the *Bermuda II* where Jack was still enjoying the remains of the bottle of wine.

A short time later, M. Gérard came to the boat and after a brief investigation, diagnosed that we had a plastic bag stuck somewhere in the cooling system. Leaving instructions with Jack on what was to be done, he bade us 'Good afternoon' and returned to his office.

Jack laboured all afternoon, and finally finished around 6.00 p.m. After dismantling what appeared to me, to be a substantial portion of the water cooling system, he announced that he had been successful in blowing the bag back through the hull opening with a high pressure hose. I was very pleased that after such a relatively short time the work had been done with such speed and efficiency. Somewhat foolishly, I suggested that we celebrate with a drink.

We were still celebrating at 9.30 p.m. Having not eaten anything since lunchtime, and as diplomatically as possible, I suggested that it was time to bring the proceedings to a close. Jack reluctantly grasped the fact that dinner was not on offer and left the boat, assuring us that he would return in the morning to make sure that everything was in order with the engine cooling system.

'Just a quick run up and down the river, and you should be on your way,' were his final words as he made his way unsteadily along the pontoon.

We were very tired, and after a quick supper, we fell asleep safe in the knowledge, that pending a successful run on the river in the morning we would soon be on our way south to the Mediterranean.

The early morning cruise on the river did not produce the result that we were hoping for. The starboard engine continued to overheat. We moored the boat to a quay on the river, and a short time later, M. Gérard returned to the boat by car and produced some scuba diving gear from the back of the car. After diving under the boat he resurfaced triumphantly waving a medium sized clear plastic bag in his hand.

'Stuck between the outside grid and the inlet,' he informed us. On our second run up and down the river the temperature gauge on the starboard engine remained in the 'Normal' position. Our problem was at last solved.

We motored back into the Gare d'eau, and while I tidied up in the engine room, Antoinette visited the nearby Casino supermarket to purchase a few supplies. We had noticed the English narrowboat *Rosie* moored up alongside a finger pontoon not far from our berth and we had exchanged the normal 'Good morning' and 'Good afternoon' salutations with the owners Roy and Audrey Brooks on our frequent trips along the pontoon. As I was busy putting away the last of the tools Roy tapped on the hull and invited us both over to *Rosie*, later in the afternoon for tea. We had never been on board an English narrowboat before, so the invitation was readily accepted. That afternoon, we were enchanted by the immaculate interior of *Rosie* where, by necessity, everything was in miniature.

Instead of leaving the next day, we took advantage of the train service to Dijon and spent a very pleasant day in the historic city, before returning late in the day, to St. Jean-de-Losne. We were becoming increasingly aware that there was a lot to see in the surrounding area, and that it would be foolish not to spend a little more time in the district before continuing our journey south. We discussed the possibility of making St. Jean-de-Losne our winter base. The proximity of the excellent Casino supermarket, post office, restaurants and Maison de la Presse, together with the friendly inhabitants of St. Jean-de-Losne, made it a very attractive proposition.

The day after my birthday, on September 15th, we were joined by an American couple, Mike and Sue Huffman, aboard their sloop *Hale Kai*. They were on passage from the Mediterranean to the North Sea and intended just a brief overnight stay. A week later, they were still moored up in the Gare d'eau!

My estimation as to the suitability of St. Jean-de-Losne for winter moorings, was further enhanced by the arrival of the *Avonbay* with celebrated waterways author Hugh McKnight at the helm. Antoinette wondered what on earth was going on as I shot out of the saloon late one afternoon, and stood by on one of the finger pontoons to take the lines, and to assist the *Avonbay* in securing alongside. Mr. McKnight was a little taken aback when I accused him of being half the reason that I was now travelling the canals of France. A look of apprehension was replaced by smiles, as I explained that we had been avid readers of his books, and that his enthusiasm on waterway travel had fueled my dreams over the years. I was delighted when he agreed to come on board the *Bermuda II* for drinks the following evening. When I told Antoinette of this, she could hardly believe that she was about to meet the man who, unbeknown to him, had become a major driving force in our lives. Over drinks, we found Hugh to be a delightful person and wished that he could have stayed longer, but prior arrangements for dinner with friends prevented this. We learnt that the *Avonbay* would be wintered in St. Jean-de-Losne, and it would not be until late March that Hugh would return.

Our plans took another turn when we received a letter from our longtime friends David and Barbie Lowe, who lived in Australia. They would be attending their daughters wedding in Switzerland on the 24th of September, and wondered if there was any way that we could get together. Their letter proved to be the turning point in our expectations to winter in the south of France. We were already booked to fly back to Bermuda on October 8th, for a three week visit, and the chances of finding a better place to leave the boat than St. Jean-de-Losne were slim indeed. The decision was made. The *Bermuda II* would remain in St. Jean-de-Losne for the winter of 1990.

Chapter 11

CHRISTMAS IN BURGUNDY

November/December 1990

We returned from Bermuda on the 5th of November and settled in for our first Christmas in France. The boat had been looked after by H₂O and apart from one small leak from the ventilator above the dinette table, everything seemed to be in good shape after being left uninhabited for a month. Our American friends, Mike and Sue, from Seattle, had been living on board their boat the *Hale Kai* which was moored to an adjacent finger pontoon. They had helped by keeping our battery banks charged and had generally kept a personal eye on things in our absence.

The day after our return, the Bourgogne sun shone in a cloudless, sky. Above the silent islands in the Gare d'eau, black crows wheeled, circled and called mournfully to one another against the backdrop of trees that stood stark and tall, stripped of their summer leaves. The wild ducks, with a sixth sense of an impending freeze, retreated to the swift flowing Saône river. No longer were the early mornings punctuated by the raucous call of the drakes seeking out their mates.

The boats, lined up in military precision alongside the finger pontoons, seemed to huddle as if additional warmth could be obtained by herding together. The misty, frosty mornings and freezing cold nights, necessitated the use of our diesel fired central heating system which proved to be wonderfully efficient.

On Wednesday the 7th of November, I managed to contact our friends, Tony Siese and Tom Trimingham in Bermuda, via amateur

Snowed in at St. Jean-de-Losne.

radio and I requested that they let the family know that we had returned safely to St. Jean-de-Losne. Radio conditions had been excellent, so we chatted away for quite some time. Because of the time difference between Bermuda and France it was well after midnight before we got to bed that night.

Sunday morning brought quite a surprise. Getting out of bed, I made my way forward to the galley to put on the morning coffee. Half way across the saloon I was suddenly conscious that everything was bathed in a soft white light. Turning around, I looked towards the aft windows which normally gave an uninterrupted view over the aft deck. The windows were covered in white stuff! Sliding open the saloon starboard side door, I was dumbfounded to see that the decks were covered with about twelve inches of snow. This was not supposed to happen so far south!

Later in the day, the locals were anxious to assure us that this was most unusual and not for seven years had St. Jean-de-Losne had snow that actually stayed on the ground for any length of time.

Mid morning a fusilade of snowballs peppered the superstructure of the boat. Peering out through the saloon windows, I could see a group of our friends taking 'pot shots' at *Bermuda II* and shouting to us to come ashore and join them in the snow. This we did, and like a group of happy children proceeded to make two large, and somewhat obscene snowmen in the parking space outside the offices of H_2O. Once the snowmen had been completed, Antoinette and I were seized from behind and rolled over and over in the soft fresh snow alongside the now semi-frozen Gare d'eau. Laughing and joking, everyone took a perverse delight in introducing two Bermudians to the joys of a French winter.

With the initiation ritual completed, we gratefully accepted an invitation from our friends David and Jena for a warming cup of coffee on board their barge the *Lena*. As we slowly thawed out, we discussed our plans for Christmas dinner and we eventually decided to seek advice from Patricia Gérard. Our prime concern was the purchase of a turkey for the Christmas dinner table as we were to be joined by our son, and Christmas without a turkey could not be contemplated, such was his love for the festive bird. Patricia told us that the only way to get a really good turkey was to purchase a live bird from the weekly poultry market in Louhans located about fifty kilometres away. She suggested that we accompany her in the car on the following Monday, which would be the 17th of December. We quickly accepted her kind invitation as it would be an ideal chance to see the surrounding countryside and also to have someone available to help us out with our very meagre French.

Louhans is well known in the Burgundy area for its weekly poultry market and not far away is the town of Bourg-en-Bresse, famous throughout France for its free-range chickens, known as Louhannaise poultry, and whose distinctive flavour is much sought after by gourmet chefs. The town of Louhans, itself, boasts a population of only 4,000 people but in summer this number is swollen by hundreds of tourists visiting the picturesque little town situated on the banks of the River Seille and dominated by its ancient church and turreted square tower.

We arrived in Louhans at 9.00 a.m. and after finding a parking place for the car we soon found ourselves in the market area where row upon row of vendors stood guard over wooden crates that contained just about every conceivable fowl—ducks, geese, chickens, guinea fowl, turkeys, pheasants and quail, to name but a few.

After wandering up and down the lines of expectant and persuasive vendors, we ended up with a lively healthy looking turkey for a very reasonable price of 100 francs (£10.00). Patricia purchased both a turkey and a huge, docile, grey goose. The birds were sold straight from the display pens so with Antoinette carrying one turkey, Patricia the other, and I, tucking the heavy grey goose under one arm, we proceeded along ancient icy streets to the car where the birds were put safely into crates for the drive back to St. Jean-de-Losne.

It was bitterly cold and we quickly agreed with Patricia's suggestion that we seek out a café for a cup of hot chocolate or coffee. The town was alive with the hustle and bustle of market day shoppers. In the main street, where the shops hide under magnificent medieval stone arches, we quickly found a café that was doing a roaring trade selling pastries and hot drinks.

With noses streaming, and flushed pink cheeks, we entered the warm and snug interior of the cafe. The aroma of fresh ground coffee hung in the air and intermingled with the sweet aroma of *pain au chocolat* whose mouth watering buttery taste, and thin strip of chocolate through the middle, had quickly become a favourite of mine.

Afterwards, suitably refreshed, we wandered around looking at the brightly lit shop windows. Outside of many shops, small Christmas trees, decorated with simple bows of red and gold ribbon, would remain day and night for the duration of the Christmas season.

The giving of Christmas gifts is not practised in France on quite the same scale as we might do in Bermuda. Instead of wildly expensive, and sometimes overly indulgent gifts, the French prefer, instead, to concentrate on purchasing succulent morsels for the Christmas day family feast. Oysters, from Bouzigues on the Mediterranean coast, ham from Bayonne, and live purple spiny sea urchins that looked as if they could have been gleaned from Bermuda's blue waters, were in great demand. Here, too, as in St. Jean-de-Losne, a huge, wild, black boar hung by its rear legs from a hook outside the local butcher's door, attracting much attention and advertising that wild boar meat was now available.

The French decorate their Christmas trees in a simple, yet artistic manner, and a large crowd of shoppers were gathered around a shop that was selling handmade Christmas tree ornaments. Delicately carved wooden sleighs, glass snow flakes, and half walnut shells containing a miniature Madonna and child, all hung with bright red ribbons, were much in demand.

Back in St. Jean-de-Losne later that morning, we constructed suitable temporary accommodation for the turkeys and the grey goose, out of chicken wire and lengths of scrap lumber. After making sure that they had enough water and grain, the birds were left to await their fate.

Our son, Michael, arrived in Dijon on the 21st of December, after a journey from Paris on the TGV, the pride of the French railway system. He would be spending ten days with us before returning to Bermuda and continuing his career in telecommunications. We collected him from the railway station in a car loaned to us by Charles Gérard. The car was of very uncertain vintage and equally uncertain reliability, but it was infinitely better than having to pay a very expensive two-way taxi fare. Later in the week, we broke the world record for a reverse push start of less than a car's length, in the centre of Beaune, on a very busy Saturday morning! We drove back to St. Jean-de-Losne across a surrealistic landscape, blanketed by fresh snow; only the black winding country road contrasted with the white moon-like vista. We passed by a small vineyard and the pruned roots stuck out of the snow like missshapened clenched fists holding the promise of new growth tightly within their grasp.

By this time, the locals were telling us that this was the worst winter in thirty years. We had no reason not to believe them.

A few days before Christmas, Patricia suggested that it would be more enjoyable if all the 'boat people' in the marina were to join together for Christmas dinner. The ten of us who insisted on waiting out the winter aboard our boats were all invited to join with the Gérard family aboard their barge the *Amicita*. It was agreed that we would pool our resources and enjoy the celebration together. Patricia came around to each boat and from one hat made us select a name, and from another had us select our contribution to the Christmas meal. We had already agreed to donate our turkey, so we were asked to bring a tray of canapés, enough for fourteen people, for pre-dinner drinks. We were also to bring a small 'fun' gift for the person whose name we had drawn, the only rule being that the gift was not to exceed 25 francs in value.

The grizzly business of dispatching the festive birds was left to me as no one else would even consider the job, although they all readily agreed that they were looking forward to eating the end product!

I eventually managed to convince Charles Gérard and Michael to at least assist by holding the birds steady on the execution block. After the axe had fallen on the first turkey, Charles turned a slight shade of green which seemed to remind him that he had an urgent telephone call to make to a client. Michael, who was wearing a brand new pair of Reeboks, was disgusted at the sight of a few specks of blood on his pristine shoes. He promptly retreated to the *Bermuda II* for what turned out to be the longest shoe cleaning exercise that I have ever known. Antoinette took on the time consuming job of plucking all three birds in an adjacent barn—well out of sight of the wood shed where the birds had been garrisoned in the equivalent of turkey death row.

Max Gérard, who was about 7 years old, had no qualms about inspecting and handling the plucked livestock. In fact he took me by complete surprise when I found him standing on a chair, next to the sink, in Patricia's kitchen where the grey goose was lying on a wooden cutting board.

'Hey! Tony. Listen to this,' he said as he grasped the goose with one hand either side of the carcass. As he squeezed, air was expelled through the vocal cords and a mighty 'honk' was heard. Laughing delightedly at his mother's disgust, the little terror was chased from the kitchen.

At 5.00 p.m. on Christmas Day, we picked our way gingerly across the ice slicked pontoon and made the short walk to the *Amicita* a 38 metre (124 feet) converted Dutch barge which is Charles and Patricia's floating home. Discarding our coats, we were immediately struck by the warmth of the interior. Charles had a blazing log fire going and the interior temperature contrasted sharply with the freezing exterior.

Most people, including us, until now, do not realize the amount of room and comfort that there is inside a 38 metre barge that has been both sensibly and sympathetically converted. Patricia's open plan kitchen is probably larger than the average house kitchen and she has all the normal appliances, including dishwasher and a full size refrigerator and freezer that one would normally associate with living on shore. The fact that we sat fourteen to Christmas dinner and still had room for more can only give an inkling as to the amount of space available.

After a magnificent dinner of turkey and roast goose with all the trimmings, Antoinette played Christmas carols on the piano and we all joined in. We were a mini United Nations: French, English, American, Bermudian, Swedish, German, Swiss and Spanish all enjoying the wonderful hospitality. Although most of the conversation was carried out in English, one could always find an interpreter if required. Charles and Patricia's daughter Jo-Jo, who was about 15 years old at the time is a good example of how the Europeans generally speak more than one language. Jo-Jo is fluent in French, English and German and makes good headway in both Spanish and Italian.

It was then time for the evening's entertainment which we had been warned about in advance. Each of us was required to perform a skit or a reading in front of the others. For several days beforehand, we had been busy on *Bermuda II* preparing for the event. Our Swedish friend Përe played the recorder, Antoinette the flute and I the guitar. Michael was pressed into service as the maracas player. The maracas were made by putting grains of rice into two empty Coca-Cola cans and sealing the holes with sticky tape. I had made up some words to a well known calypso tune that involved everyone present. With our homemade wigs of black wool dreadlocks, Bermuda shorts and baseball caps we sang a version of 'Jamaica Farewell' which had everyone laughing and joining in the well-known chorus.

It was 2.30 a.m. when we left the *Amicita* and crunching ice and snow underfoot, we walked through swirling river mist to our warm beds on *Bermuda II*. It had been a Christmas that we will both remember and cherish forever.

Chapter 12

THE CIRCUS COMES TO TOWN

April 1991

'There's a camel over by Crown Blue Line,' I announced to Antoinette one afternoon in mid April.

'Are you sure?'

'Well, I'm not sure if it's a dromedary. I can never remember which has one hump and which has two.'

'No, silly. I mean are you sure? What's an animal like that doing over at Crown Blue Line.'

'Haven't a clue. Let's go and take a look.'

Hastily leaving our pre-cruising chores of sanding, painting, varnishing and cleaning, we strolled around the Gare d'eau and joined a small group of inquisitive onlookers to see what on earth a camel was doing tied up on the grass immediately opposite the reception office of the Crown Blue Line hire boat base.

A travelling circus had come to town, and a variety of animals were being unloaded from garishly painted trailers and tethered to wooden stakes driven into the ground on the vacant lot of land adjacent to the Crown Blue Line base.

It was a very sad circus. As we wandered around the painted trailers we could see that the paint was cracked and peeling and that the condition of the animals was almost pitiful. The camel's two humps, which sagged forlornly to one side, looked like an old wool blanket that had been ravaged by a plague of moths. A once white llama, gazed cautiously at us through rheumy weeping eyes. Half a dozen timid, and hobbled ponies, munched gratefully at the lush green grass and shuffled morosely out of the way whenever they were approached by their handler.

The one exception to this lamentable sight was the trailer that contained half a dozen magnificent tigers. The paintwork of the trailer shone like a jewel and through the metal bars on the side of the trailer, we could see the lively inhabitants who appeared to be in excellent condition.

A large, blue and white marquee, was being erected and already the wooden ticket office had been assembled and the tinny amplified voice of the ticket seller was exhorting the public to purchase tickets in advance for the evenings performance.

For the time being we had seen enough, and we strolled back to the boat debating, while we walked, the virtues of returning for the evening show. After some consideration we decided that our social calendar was not too full so we would attend the 7.00 p.m. performance.

After dinner, we walked back over to the circus site, and joined the end of the queue that was made up of about a hundred or so locals. As is often the case in France, the queue was more of a semi-organized mob than an organized procession. We eventually shouldered our way to what passed for the front of the queue and purchased two seats, for an outrageous price, in the *première chaise* section. The *première chaise* turned out to be half a dozen rickety, wooden fold-up chairs that were positioned immediately in front of the small arena.

The show commenced with a comedy routine by a clown whose red plastic bulbous nose was in the same state of disrepair as the oversized red, green and yellow painted leather boots that he wore. At the end of his act the clown left the arena, and the master of ceremonies announced that we would next be entertained by 'wild' Red Indians who would amaze us with their riding skills. With a recorded fanfare of trumpets, more suitable to Caesar's grand entrance, two riders stripped to the waist and wearing feathered headdresses, swept into the ring. I recognized the taller of the two as the clown who had obviously done a lightning character change, and was now a 'wild' Red Indian riding a pony with no saddle. After a dozen or so circuits of the arena, accompanied by much whooping and waving of plastic tomahawks, they made their exit and the master of ceremonies told us that it was now time for the main event. There was to be a brief pause while a steel cage was erected in the arena in order to protect the public from the ferocious tigers. The cage was swiftly erected and this time I noticed that the clown had hastily donned a pair of blue overalls, which together with his war painted face, made him look quite bizarre.

With yet another recorded fanfare the tigers rushed into the ring and obediently sat on the high stools around the perimeter of the cage. The animal trainer, who thankfully was not the clown, appeared wearing a suit of electric-blue, sequined stretch Lycra and was armed with the traditional long rawhide whip. Each crack of the whip brought an appropriate bored snarl from the beast at which it was aimed. Once again, we commented to each other how well looked after the tigers appeared to be, in comparison with the rest of the animals.

The tigers performed all the usual stunts of rolling over in unison, leaping through flaming rings and walking upright on their hind legs, when all of a sudden it happened. A male tiger, after finishing his party piece in the centre of the arena returned to his high stool, and, with its rear end on to the cage, raised his tail and shot a stream of urine through the bars and onto the spectators sitting in the *première chaise*. Poor Antoinette was in the direct line of fire and received a large helping all over her glasses and her hair. The crowd roared with laughter and Antoinette, wiping the substance from her glasses with a tissue, could not help but join in with a disgusted laugh.

We stuck it through to the end of the show in spite of the aroma and being plunged into darkness on a couple of occasions when the portable generator either ran out of fuel or malfunctioned. After a grand parade of all the dilapidated looking animals we beat a hasty retreat back to the boat where Antoinette plunged herself into a hot shower.

'No more circuses for me,' she said as she vigorously dried her hair with a towel.

'That's the first, and the last,' she said, making reference to the fact that coming from a small island like Bermuda, she had never seen a circus in her life before. We also realized that our attendance had condoned the ghastly way in which the animals were kept and treated. We were 'off' circuses for good. However, we were still giggling to ourselves about the unusual, and rather smelly event, when we turned in for the night.

The next morning, I strolled up to the office of H_2O in order to check for any mail that might have arrived for us. Half way to the office I was greeted by Hugo and Hot Dog, Charles and Patricia's two large dogs of dubious Rhodesian ridgeback parentage, who between them were the canine terrors and masters of the Gare d'eau. Both dogs had grown accustomed to my daily office visit and would come bounding up to me to see if I was carrying any scraps or bones that might have been left over from our previous night's dinner. The younger of the two dogs, Hot Dog, approached me with his usual gangling gait and wagging tail. All of a sudden he stood motionless, and then sniffing the air and extending his muzzle in slow motion, cautiously zeroed in on the cuff of my trousers. As a look of disbelief crept into his eyes I suddenly realized that maybe I had not been as fortunate as I had previously thought in evading the tiger's unwelcome stream. Clearly a few drops had succeeded in dousing my trouser cuff. With the very tip of Hot Dog's nose quivering about two inches from my trouser leg, I let out the loudest imitation tiger's roar that I could muster.

The effect on Hot Dog was quite startling. The poor dog rolled his eyes heavenwards until only the whites were showing, which resulted in him loosing his balance and falling sideways in an almost dead swoon. It was one of the funniest things that I have ever seen and I burst out laughing. Hot Dog quickly recovered his senses, stood up, and promptly relieved himself on my trouser leg. Now that we were more or less even, he cast an anxious look over his shoulder and went bounding away home to the *Amicita*. I returned to the boat, and still chuckling, handed the offending pair of trousers to Antoinette, with a request that they be washed as soon as possible. In a way, I guess that I was very fortunate as a more belligerent dog than Hot Dog might well have bitten my ankle off!

Chapter 13

 St. Jean-de-Losne to Épernay
328.4 kilometres, 133 locks

April 27th, 1991

The fickle weather of March slowly gave way to a glorious April and as the first blush of wildflowers appeared along the banks of the River Saône, we prepared the *Bermuda II* for our second season of cruising on the French inland waterways.

The sleepy little town of St. Jean-de-Losne stirred with new life as more and more owners visited their boats on weekends, preparing for the summer cruising season. The first of the tourist hire cruisers had appeared over the Easter break which was the last weekend in March, and the frantic shouts of inexperienced skippers, as they made crash landings alongside the finger pontoons, was becoming a daily event. The sight of an approaching hire cruiser was enough to put the more permanent residents of the marina on red alert and would send them scurrying to help with the mooring lines, or reaching for the nearest boat hook, to fend off and protect their respective boats. Our friends, Ian and Sandy, on board their boat, *Kingfisher*, were in a particularly vulnerable spot on the outer pontoon, and poor Sandy seemed to spend more time with a boathook in her hand than with the cushion covers that she was laboriously sewing by hand.

The ducks and swans reappeared from their nesting places on the river and noisily demanded scraps for themselves and their newly hatched offspring. We identified each family of ducks according to the number of ducklings that they had in tow. The tiny ducklings, if startled, would propel themselves across the water at great speed like fuzzy ping-pong balls blown across the water. Mrs 'Seven', 'Eight' or 'Nine' would appear each morning and afternoon with a frequency that hinted of conspiracy between them.

We had planned an ambitious and extensive cruise which would take us north, on the Canal de la Marne à Saône to Épernay, west, on the River Marne to Paris, south, on the canals of the Centre and then south, on the River Rhône. We thought that the first week in May would be a suitable departure time. However, our friends, Mike and Sue, who were also planning to take the *Hale Kai* north, found out that there was to be a *chômage* or planned closure of the first lock, between the Saône and the Marne à Saône canal. The closure was to take effect at 7.30 p.m. on 28 April and it would last for two weeks. Because of this, we decided to leave St. Jean-de-Losne around lunchtime on the last day before the closure and this would give us enough time to make the forty kilometre trip past the first lock before the closure took effect.

The Canal de la Marne à la Saône covers a distance of 224 kilometres with 114 locks between Heuilley sur Saône, in the south, and Vitry-le-François, in the north. At the summit level, on the Langres plateau, the canal passes through the 4,820-metre-long Balesmes tunnel at an altitude of 340 metres (1,115 feet) above sea level. We had read that this canal, which was first opened to navigation in 1907, has few suitable stopping places, or facilities for large pleasure craft transitting the canal, and so we planned accordingly.

For two days prior to our departure, Antoinette seemed intent on stripping the local Casino supermarket of its entire stock. Looking over the array of groceries that were being stowed in the galley cabinets, it was quite apparent that whatever else happened, we were not going to starve to death.

With enough supplies on board for a transatlantic trip, and with our water tanks filled to overflowing, we said farewell to friends that had gathered on the pontoon to see us off. We were very touched when Patricia Gérard appeared with a bouquet of flowers and a bottle of champagne to wish us *bon voyage*. Three farewell blasts were sounded on the boat's fog horn as we made our exit from the Gare d'eau which had been our home for the past five months.

We made our way upstream on the River Saône, cruising at a sedate pace and taking in the beauty of the river banks, in their spring foliage.

Past fields of bright yellow Rape.

Timid, grey herons would stand as motionless as sentinels on stilt-like legs until we approached to within a hundred or so metres of their bankside fishing pools. They would then rise languidly into the air, only to settle a short distance upstream where the whole process would be repeated many times over.

Shortly after 4.00 p.m. we passed through the first two canal locks and found a suitable mooring spot just upstream of Lock 42 (Maxilly) where we decided that we would spend the night. We were now above the planned *chômage* and we were in no desperate hurry. The mooring was peaceful and with only the sound of the birds, and the occasional car passing far in the distance, it was quite a contrast from the clatter of feet on the busy pontoons at St. Jean-de-Losne.

The next day was a Sunday and as the locks do not operate on Sundays on this particular canal we had a fairly lazy day. Prior to our departure from St. Jean-de-Losne, we had been given two ancient, but serviceable bicycles by our friends, David and Jena, so while I repaired a couple of punctures and did a few mechanical adjustments, Antoinette started the generator and vacuumed through the boat.

On Monday morning, we set off upstream after breakfast and we quickly found out that our long winter sojourn in St. Jean-de-Losne had reduced both our fitness and our boat handling skills. Cranking the lock gate mechanism seemed far more strenuous than I remembered, and Antoinette's double handed line throwing, which had previously been expertly executed, missed more bollards on the first attempt than she would care to admit.

It was a bright sunny day and the canal wound its way through remote countryside, cutting through fields of bright yellow rape in full bloom, a yellow, so bright that it made the eyes ache and it seemed to light up the surrounding countryside with a primrose coloured glow.

At the end of the day, we were both quite tired and after having passed through twenty locks, our skills were beginning to regain their former glory. It was just after 6.15 p.m. when we stopped for the night, a little upstream of Lock 22 (Cussey) and once again the peace and quiet of the countryside was delightful.

Over dinner, we commented on the various locks that we had passed through during the day and that the lock keepers, by an large, did not seem to be overly friendly. One lock keeper had even conducted the whole locking process without a word, or so much as a glance at either us, or the boat, a feat that must have required some practice. At another lock, we waited patiently for half an hour for the lock keeper to appear. The eventual 'toot' on the boat's horn aroused an obviously very pregnant lady who was not very happy at our disturbance of her afternoon siesta. The RSPCA would have been proud of the lock that was literally crawling with cats of all shapes, sizes and colours. We counted up to thirty cats, before we gave up; none of them had learnt to stand still long enough for a head count to be taken. The lady who was in charge of the lock, said that she, herself, was not quite sure of the exact number. Smiling broadly, to reveal a set of teeth, somewhat akin to a burnt fence, she shrugged her shoulders and continued with the locking process.

The barometer had been falling slowly for the past few days so it was no surprise when Tuesday ushered itself in with overcast, chilly conditions and light rain showers. We cast off, hoping that the weather might improve as the day went on and as we continued our slow progress upstream. The locks were quite close together so there was no opportunity to spend any length of time inside the boat and out of the rain. By lunchtime, we were cold and wet. It was apparent that the weather was not going to improve so when a convenient quay appeared in the small village of Villeguisien, we quickly agreed that we had done enough cruising for the day. We had only covered twenty-four kilometres but we had passed through thirteen locks and this meant that we had only another eight locks to pass through, before we reached the summit level of the canal. It was our intention to spend only one night alongside in Villeguisien but we found out that the next day, May 1st, was a public holiday and the locks would therefore be closed to navigation.

In the morning, although the rain had stopped it was still quite cold and damp. Antoinette had visited the local village shop the previous evening and had decided that the proper way to start the day off in such conditions was with a breakfast of good, old-fashioned porridge. The shop sold just about everything from groceries to pots, pans, galvanized buckets, gardening tools, egg incubators, children's toys and electric fencing. She had purchased a packet of oats, which from appearances, looked to be the same as Quaker Oats. The porridge that appeared at the breakfast table bore little resemblance to anything that we had ever seen or tasted before.

'This stuff is disgusting,' I said, holding my spoon in mid air and observing the glutinous, grey-white lump that clung tenaciously to the spoon.

'Yes, it is a bit strange. Perhaps I should have soaked it first.'

'Too bad we finished wall papering the loo.'

'Why's that?'

'Make great wall paper paste,' I said, looking at the spoon that was now defying gravity by remaining vertical in the bowl.

'I'll try again tomorrow with a different method,' Antoinette assured me. With that threat hanging over my head, I retreated to the warmth of the engine room to check the raw water filters and oil levels in the engines.

Later that day, we went for a long walk, bundled up in our winter sweaters and warm jackets. The walk was followed by a cycle ride up to the summit level to take a look at the southern entrance to the Balesmes tunnel. This proved to be a little difficult as the towpath ended about 500 metres from the entrance and necessitated a scramble through thick undergrowth. It was hardly worth the effort as from our vantage point, we could see only an unspectacular red brick entrance set in dense forest.

The next day, I was out of bed at 5.00 a.m. and by the time the coffee was ready, the pale light of dawn had just started to spread across the landscape. Plumes of mist skimmed across the surface of the water in an early morning silent ballet, driven by a slight easterly breeze. Today, we would pass through the Balesmes tunnel and because of the one way system that was in effect, we wanted to catch the north bound opening time that would last until 9.00 a.m. Failure to enter the tunnel before 9.00 a.m. would mean waiting a whole day for the next north bound schedule at 8.00 p.m.

At 6.35 a.m. we entered the first of the eight automatic locks that lead to the summit level. Between locks 5 and 6, and again between locks 2 and 3, we met unladen barges heading downstream but the width of the passing pounds allowed us to pass them with room to spare.

Just past the small village of Heuilley Cotton, we entered the 4,820 metre long tunnel. The interior of the tunnel was musty, warm and humid, so humid, in fact, that it caused my glasses to fog up in the first twenty metres. The tunnel was not lit but once Antoinette had adjusted our twin searchlights, we could clearly see the way ahead. It was impossible to see any light at the distant end of the tunnel and staring down the twin shafts of light, and concentrating on keeping the *Bermuda II* central in the narrow waterway, quickly led to slight disorientation. Shadows and reflections sometimes created the illusion of obstructions and at one point in time, I felt sure that the tunnel was actually turning a corner which was impossible as we knew that the tunnel was as straight as an arrow.

At 9.30 a.m. we emerged from the tunnel and we were greeted by dull overcast weather that was doing its very best to rain but could only produce a few light sprinkles. It had taken us one hour and ten minutes to transit the tunnel and it remains the longest tunnel that we ever passed through on our extensive inland cruising.

By mid-morning we were tied up alongside a decaying stone and wood quay from where we could clearly see the hillside town of Langres, about two kilometres away. After lunch, we decided to tackle the steep, uphill climb and we spent the rest of the afternoon wandering around the busy streets of Langres. The town has strong Romano–Gallic connections but only a disfigured gateway survives from that period. There are a few ancient buildings, notably the chapel of

Amoncourt and the church of Saint-Martin which was well worth a visit, but for me the breathtaking view from the renovated ramparts overlooking the broad plateau below was well worth the long uphill walk.

After another three days of travelling northwards, we were approaching the town of St. Dizier and we were running perilously low on our fresh water supplies. We had been unable to top up our tanks since leaving St. Jean-de-Losne, nine days earlier, so it was a considerable relief when we were offered the garden hose at Lock 55 (Chamlouilley). The lady lock keeper, who must have been familiar with the dearth of facilities for pleasure craft on the Marne à la Saône, stopped the locking process and chatted happily away while we replenished our dwindling water supply. After giving her a small tip, we thanked her and cruised slowly through the commercial, dismal looking, town of St. Dizier. The pleasure port, on the downstream outskirts of the town, was very small and we were fortunate in finding a space that would just accommodate the length and breadth of the *Bermuda II*.

Once moored in the port, the proprietor produced a length of heavy duty electrical cable which we joined to our own extensive cable, and which enabled us to connect with the shore electricity supply. This was of great help as the generator had started acting up and would run only under protest. Blissfully, we availed ourselves of two very long and very hot showers!

We had designated St. Dizier as a pick-up point for mail and a quick check at the poste restante facility of the main post office produced nothing. We then realized that we would have to remain in St. Dizier longer than we had planned and, as the next two days were public holidays, it would be Friday at the earliest before we could expect any mail. We decided to kill time by taking a train ride up to Épernay the next day, to see if Mike and Sue aboard the *Hale Kai* were berthed there, and at the same time we could review the pleasure boat facilities that were available in Épernay. On our way north, we had asked various lock keepers if they had seen the *Hale Kai* and we concluded from their information that prior to our arrival in St. Dizier, we had been catching them up and had reduced the deficit from one week to one day. I felt sure that they would be in Epernay and I looked forward to surprising them with an unexpected visit.

The railway station in Épernay is only a short walk away from the

Canal de la Marne à la Saône. Delays at various locks.

Club Nautique d'Épernay. Although it is a privately owned club, we had read that it extends a warm welcome to pleasure craft transitting the canal. Upon arrival at the club, we were disappointed to see that the *Hale Kai* was not moored alongside but we were delighted to meet John Collard, who together with his Norfolk Broads-style cruiser is more or less a permanent fixture at the club. John's reputation as a knowledgeable, and accurate source of information on the waterways, had reached St. Jean-de-Losne where Sandy and Ian had shown us some of his extensive handwritten notes. John informed us that he had not seen the *Hale Kai* but that he would be sure to mention our visit to Mike and Sue should they turn up. We were subsequently to learn that they had indeed arrived the very next day and that they had remained in Épernay for a couple of days, expecting our arrival. Unfortunately, we had to wait longer in St. Dizier than we had expected for the mail to arrive, and they had continued on their way into Holland via the Canal des Ardennes.

Our mail eventually arrived on Monday, and it was not long after when we were once again cruising between fields of brilliant, yellow rape, on our way towards Vitry-le-François. The canal was absolutely straight as far as the eye could see and after the first six locks, it became quite uninteresting. It was with some relief, therefore, when we eventually arrived in Vitry-le-François and found a suitable quay just a few metres away from the small pleasure port.

We had intended to make the cruise from Vitry-le-François to Épernay in just one day but there was a lot of commercial traffic on the Canal Latéral à la Marne. As a result, the sight of a pleasure boat pontoon, in the tiny village of Mareuil-sur-Ay, enticed us to pull over and stop for the night. We were only a short distance from Épernay and we had plenty of time in hand before we were due to pick up my cousin Marjorie and her husband Alan who would be joining us for a cruising holiday of one week.

The following day, the weather which for the past couple of days had been pretty miserable, improved considerably and after lunch, we left Mareuil sur Ay in bright sunshine. We cruised alongside hundreds of acres of vine clad slopes that surround Épernay. These vineyards provide the grapes for some of the best known champagne in the world and we were suitably impressed by the sheer size and extent of the viniculture.

Arriving at the Club Nautique d'Épernay we were greeted by John Collard who gave us the bad news that we had missed Mike and Sue by just four days. This was a great disappointment as we had very much enjoyed each other's company while in St. Jean-de-Losne.

We were delighted with the hospitality and the facilities that the Club Nautique extended to us and apart from the closeness of the railway line, and the resulting early morning train noises, it was an ideal base for exploring Épernay. The centre of the town and the Avenue de Champagne was just a five minute cycle ride away so we were able to make good use of our two old bikes while we explored the town and awaited the arrival of Marjorie and Alan.

Chapter 14

ÉPERNAY

May 21st/26th, 1991

Even the briefest of walks around this interesting city can only confirm the fact that one is at the heart of the champagne industry. Along the Avenue des Champagne, one notices names that are so famous that they have almost become household words. The giants of the champagne producers such as, Moët et Chandon, Mercier, Pol Roger and others rub shoulders with those of lesser international fame.

It is only after a guided tour of any of the well known champagne 'houses' can one begin to comprehend the fact that in the caves beneath Épernay rest millions of bottles of some of the finest champagnes that France has to offer. We took John Collard's advice, and early one morning, we joined the guided tour of the prestigious Moët et Chandon caves. Visitors to the building enter through a wrought iron encircled courtyard, under the gaze of monk Dom Perignon's statue (1638-1715) who is credited with the distinction of being the first person to produce champagne.

The tour guide did her very best to answer questions but in the end, we felt that the mystique of champagne making remained an almost top secret affair. It was not until the afternoon when we toured the Castellane factory and caves, that we actually got to see the interesting bottling process, and to view the unglamorous vast stainless steel vats where the champagne is stored prior to bottling. Large hoses, not unlike those one might expect to find on a fire truck, snaked their way across the tiled floor, and precious champagne ran

Épernay—Champagne bottling.

in rivulets down tiled waste gutters. The noisy, clattering bottling machine was a modern scientific wonder and the blue overall clad workers contrasted sharply with our *haute couture* tour of Moët et Chandon. Both of the tours were very interesting and educational, and they allowed us to see two different aspects of champagne production and naturally enough they were one of the highlights of our stay in Épernay.

Another highlight was a truely memorable luncheon at the Steam Boat Restaurant located at 5 Rue de Rcims, where the seafood was superbly cooked and presented in style. The huge hors-d'oeuvre platter of shrimps, mussels, crab, oysters, prawns and bulots (somewhat akin to a large periwinkle) served on a bed of crushed ice resting on a silver platter and accompanied by a variety of interesting sauces, was outstanding.

No trip to Épernay would be complete unless one came away with some champagne. Our biggest problem was to decide which particular brand we liked the best. We eventually solved the problem in a delightful way by purchasing a mixed box of eight half bottles, and over the next few days we religiously sampled each bottle in turn. We were a little surprised at our eventual choice of Mercier which for our taste came out on top. Almost all of the Mercier champagne is consumed by the French, with very little finding its way overseas. Were the daily baguettes and ample portions of charcuterie subversively acting on our nationality?

We consulted with John Collard before going ahead with our purchase and it was just as well that we did so. John suggested that we visit the proprietor of a small wine and grocery establishment hidden away in a small side street off the main square. John assured us that we would find there the best prices in town and upon investigation, this proved to be true. In a small shop that seemed to have a little of everything for sale and reeked of strong cheeses, we struck a bargain with Madame, the proprietor. At one stage of the bargaining I did however place the whole deal in jeopardy by suggesting to Madame that a further ten per cent reduction, of her already low prices, might be in order. Snapping shut her notebook, she almost growled at me that I should go and see if I could do any better somewhere else. I hastily reconsidered and apologized for my indiscretion.

The next morning, the *Bermuda II* took delivery of a case and a half of champagne which was stored beneath the bunks in the middle cabin and would be reserved for special occasions. With the movement of the boat, and the vibration, I suppose that it was not the best way to store champagne, but we had no intention of being frugal in declaring 'special occasions'.

On Sunday, I rigged up the wire dipole antenna which was proving to be wonderfully efficient for my regular amateur radio schedules with friends back in Bermuda. One end of the wire was secured to a telescoping aluminium mast which had to be rigged on the fore deck, and the other end of the wire was secured rather crudely to the boat hook which I lashed to the aft safety rail. Due to the height of the telescoping mast, and the number of low bridges that we had to pass under, it was impossible to rig the mast and the antenna as a permanent fixture. With Antoinette's help, the whole arrangement could be ready for service in about five minutes, and if radio conditions were good we would usually talk to our friends in Bermuda for an hour or more. It was an ideal, and fun way to keep in touch with island events and on this occasion I could almost hear the groans of envy when I told our amateur radio friends that we were sitting right in the middle of the French Champagne country. There are some things

Épernay. Moored up alongside the Club Nautique.

that you can say, and some things that you can't say on amateur radio, and on this occasion their replies were not strictly in accordance with the rule book!

A day later we were joined at the Club Nautique by an American couple, Bruce and Kincey Potter, who were on six months sabbatical leave from their work in Washington D.C. They were touring the canals on a hire cruiser and it came as no surprise when they told us that they were enchanted with the canals and rivers of France. Over drinks, I remarked that I was envious of their two very smart mountain bikes which they had brought with them from America and made our two old clunkers look like museum pieces by comparison.

'Too bad that we were not meeting you at the end of our stay in France,' said Bruce. 'It's our intention to sell them, before we go back home.' I, too thought that it was a pity, but little did I know then, that as fate would have it, we would eventually end up owning the same two cycles.

Chapter 15

ÉPERNAY TO PARIS
187.2 KILOMETRES, 18 LOCKS

May 27th/30th, 1991

My cousin Marjorie and her husband Alan, arrived in Épernay by train on Saturday, and in addition to their gifts of two beautiful sweaters, they also brought with them a stack of mail that they had been holding for us pending their visit. There were a few nasty looking window envelopes that would have to be attended to before our departure. The delay would give our guests a couple of days to enjoy some sightseeing around Épernay, before starting out on our cruise down the River Marne. I had completely forgotten that the boat insurance was due at the end of the month and that it would have to be taken care of, before we could contemplate continuing on our way. Unlike other forms of insurance, marine insurance allows no period of grace so the premium has to be paid on time.

Monday, 27th May, brought with it a bright and clear morning and after saying our farewells to Gino, the affable *guardien* of the Club Nautique, and John Collard, we cast off and proceeded downstream on the River Marne past lines of pollarded trees that were beginning to sprout with their summer foliage. The hillside slopes, around the little town of Cumières, were heavily planted with grape vines and the green fuzz of new growth was already in evidence as we cruised slowly past.

The first lock of the day, just past Cumières, was quite a large lock and had sloping sides. Rather unusually, metal posts had been driven into the floor of the lock and offset from the centre, which meant that we were able to moor up in the conventional fore and aft manner, during the locking process. By 3.00 p.m. we had travelled some fifty kilometres down the Marne and were on the outskirts of Château-Thierry where we planned to stop for the night. Our early arrival gave us a choice of vacant moorings and ample time to explore the town, but our search for a suitable restaurant for dinner was in vain. Every restaurant in town seemed to be taking an extended Whit Sunday holiday and the only establishment that was open, yielded the worst meal that we have ever had in France. There was no choice of menu and while the pâté en croûte was passable, the main course was terrible. Two large, boiled, German sausages defied all nautical theory by staying afloat on a limpid pool of green lentils. The overall result both looked and tasted disgusting. Fortunately, we all kept our sense of humour and we vowed that we would treat ourselves to a real dinner at our next port of call.

The next day, after a very pleasant and uneventful cruise, our gastronomic expectations were fulfilled when we had an excellent meal at the restaurant Château Marysied in the little town of Mary-sur-Marne.

Our overnight moorings would have been idyllic had it not been for the railway bridge, about 100 metres away, where the first commuter train of the day roused us from our slumbers at dawn. Shortly after the train's passage, a repair gang took over the percussion section by busily chipping the paint off the steel bridge with compressed air tools. As further sleep was impossible, we left the now noisy moorings early and retreated to the peace and quiet of the river, cruising through pleasant farm land and tree lined river banks.

At Meaux, which has been famous for its production of Brie cheese since the early thirteenth century, we had a slight delay caused by commercial traffic proceeding through the lock to the Canal de Meaux à Chalifert. Once we were allowed through the lock, we quickly caught up with the barge that had preceded us and as the canal was narrow, we resigned ourselves to plodding along behind it, through some flat, and not very interesting countryside. We were delayed even further at Chalifert before we were released through the lock on to the comparatively wide River Marne once again.

This section of the river carried quite a lot of commercial traffic and we were kept on our toes by the considerable amount of 'blue flagging' that was being done by barges travelling upstream. Craft

The Port de Plaisance, Paris Arsenal.

passing each other in opposite directions normally keep to their starboard side of the waterway, but sometimes, due to either shoals, current or river bends, barges display a rectangular blue painted board outside the wheelhouse to indicate that they wish to pass on the opposite side to normal. By night, and in poor visibility a white flashing light is displayed in the centre of the blue board and woe betide the pleasure craft skipper who ignores this request.

We made good time on the river, weaving in and out of the barges, and it was not long before we were waiting outside the last lock that connects the River Marne to the River Seine at Maisons Alfort. This lock proved to be a major bottleneck. We waited for an hour and a half for the endless convoy of preferentially treated commercial traffic to pass through the lock, and then we were finally able to enter and proceed downstream on the River Seine.

It was a glorious afternoon, and as we approached the first of the famous Paris bridges, I turned the wheel over to Antoinnette and disappeared below. I had previously hidden a bottle of Mercier champagne and four glasses at the back of the fridge for just this occasion. Rejoining the others on the aft deck, I opened the bottle with a flourish and we sat sipping Mercier champagne as we passed under the bridges of Paris.

We arrived adjacent to the entrance to the Port de Plaisance, Paris Arsenal, about an hour earlier than planned, so much to everyone's delight, we had ample time to cruise downstream past the Notre Dame cathedral and on to the Eiffel Tower. I think that Alan had just about run out of film as we turned around and proceeded slowly back upstream to the reception pontoon that marked the entrance to the Port de Plaisance. It had been the type of afternoon that made our decision to embark on this two year cruise fully justified, and it remains one of our fondest memories of our French cruising adventures.

Chapter 16

Paris to Auxerre
207.2 Kilometres, 34 Locks

June 11th/18th, 1991

After a very pleasant ten days in Paris we found ourselves longing for some rural solitude. Paris is a very exciting city but, like all cities, the hustle, bustle and constant noise gets a little tedious after a while. It was time to leave.

We shopped along the Rue St. Antoine one last time, and after the last of the heavy plastic bags was deposited in the galley, I left it up to Antoinette to stow everything away. Somehow, whenever this process was taking place, I was told that I was either in the way, or for weeks later we could not locate an item which we knew we had, as I had put it in entirely the wrong place! I therefore took a quick trip on the Metro, to the Marks and Spencer store to replenish our dwindling supply of English bacon that was in the deep-freeze.

Upon my return, I paid our port dues and we proceeded through the lock to the busy River Seine.

It was a glorious June day. We cruised upriver under clear blue skies with the temperature slowly climbing into the eighties. Our departure time of 10.30 a.m. was a little later than intended and upon reflection, it would have been wiser to have left earlier. The Seine was alive with commercial traffic of every description, including many laden push-tows transporting sand and gravel in both directions. I concluded that the French have hit upon the perfect solution of how to keep the bargees in business: one fleet of barges brings the sand and gravel down to Paris, and another fleet takes it back up!

Due to the extent of the commercial traffic, we were frequently delayed in our progress upstream. Suddenly, a convoy of barges would appear from astern of us, and, having the right of way over pleasure craft, they would fill the locks to capacity, precluding the entry of any pleasure craft. At those locks that did allow enough room for us to enter, we were packed in behind the powerful push tows. We stayed firmly secured to the lockside bollards to allow the turbulence of their exit to subside, before we cast off and followed them upstream.

By 5.00 p.m. we had managed only four locks and had covered about forty-five kilometres upstream. Although we could have continued cruising until the lock closing time of 7.30 p.m. we were both nearly fried to a crisp from the sun, so we moored for the night near a disused lock at the 123 kilometre marker post. These marker posts are extremely useful for calculating the speed made good over the ground and for pin-pointing one's exact position on the waterway. Apart from the nearby railway line it was a pleasant mooring, although there were no facilities of any kind in the immediate area.

We left the River Seine at Montereau and passed beneath the road bridge that spans the junction of the River Yonne and the Seine. A short distance upstream, and directly opposite a large Gothic church, we found a small but adequate, public quay which we promptly commandeered for our overnight mooring. Over dinner on board, we discussed endless theories about how to handle the sloping sided locks of the Yonne that we would encounter in the morning. We had read much about these locks and their ability to wreak havoc with twin screwed craft. In Verdun, a year earlier, Barry from the *Atlantis* had passed on some useful tips about negotiating the Yonne locks, but he still claimed that he had not worked out the complete solution. We went to bed that night in some trepidation of what the mornings cruise would bring.

The Yonne is one of the most interesting cruising rivers in France but, as with most interesting things in life, there are also several problems. Heaven comes in the shape of the beautiful countryside and interesting villages disected by the broad river. Hell, we were to discover, comes in the shape of the sloping sided locks. Many words have been written about the Yonne locks, and I can but add a few more. I wish that I could come face-to-face tomorrow, with the engineer who designed these navigational monstrosities. I suppose that

Sloping sided lock on River Yonne.

there must be a logical reason for such a design, but if there is, the logic eludes me and I would love to hear the explanation. Upon entering a Yonne lock for the first time, two things will be apparent. The first is that the lock is of greater dimensions than the standard Freycinet locks, and the second is that due to the sloping sides, it is impossible to get a line, or a crew member ashore, if you have a twin screwed boat, to moor the boat up fore and aft in the normal fashion.

The French Navigation Authority, showing the darker side of their humour, have placed notices at the entrance to each lock informing skippers 'Amarrage Obligatoire' which is impossible unless you happen to be a dab hand at throwing a lasso. We did, on one occasion, manage to enlist the help of the lock keeper but once we had thrown him the line he stood on the lockside not knowing quite what to do with it. Obviously we were not the first people to ignore the signs! We did find out that it was possible to throw a double line over the bollard located just inside of the entry gate, and by securing the other end to our stern, and putting the engines into slow forward, we could use this line to pull against. Using this system the *Bermuda II* would stay pretty much in the centre of the lock, and was in fact Barry's favourite method.

Once the upstream paddles were opened the turbulence of the water meant that it took some skill manipulating both engines to keep us centrally located. I would advise other skippers of twin screwed craft to exercise extreme caution, as a propeller striking the stone sides can have very expensive consequences.

We made good progress through the first four sloping sided locks, and at the fifth lock, we caught up with a standard 38 metre barge pushing a 38 metre 'dumb' barge ahead of it. We hung back from the lock, thinking that we would have to wait for the next lock cycle before we were allowed to enter. Much to our amazement, we were waved in by the lock keeper and told to make fast alongside the barge. This we did, with an anxious eye on the distance between us and the sloping side. We need not have worried. In fact, it proved to be the easiest method of negotiating sloping sided locks.

The professional barge captains can handle their barges with amazing skill. While this captain did all the work of keeping both craft in the middle of the lock, Antoinette struck up a conversation with the captain's wife. We were invited on board the barge to view the very modern kitchen that Madame was obviously very proud of. The kitchen took up the whole of the aft section of the large wheelhouse, which allowed Madame to cook the meals, chat to her husband, watch the countryside go by and to be available immediately to give a hand with the lines, or the wheel, when entering and leaving locks. The kitchen, and the rest of the interior was immaculate. Due to the rather dirty canal environment, some of the commercial barges might appear to be scruffy from the outside but the interiors that we saw were always neat and clean. Once the water level in the lock had equalized, our new found friends allowed us to go ahead of them knowing that we would proceed more quickly than they would. We left them with the usual Bermuda souvenirs, and bid them *au revoir*.

Shortly after this we were subjected to a hair raising trick, commonly practised by certain Yonne lock keepers: the habit of only opening one entry, and one exit gate, thus saving the lock keeper the long walk around the perimeter of the lock. The *Bermuda II* is 14 feet of beam, and squeezing a 23 ton boat between a concrete wall on one side and a lock gate on the other, took considerable concentration, especially in a cross breeze.

At 4.30 p.m. we moored at the pleasure port in the cathedral city of Sens. An electricity point was a welcome sight as our generator had refused to start for the past few days and I had not had a chance to investigate the problem fully. The water tap was a little further away on the quay but by connecting the three fresh water hoses, that we now carried on board, we were able to replenish our tanks. Hot showers and all the fresh water that we wanted—luxury!

Sens is a very old and interesting city, and is well worth exploring. The cathedral was begun about 1130 by Archbishop Henri Sanglier. Thomas à Beckett took refuge here from King Henry II of England in 1159, finding that King Louis VII was quick to extend the hand of friendship for his own political gains. After Becket's murder, when he returned to England, the architect of Sens Cathedral was commissioned to redesign Canterbury Cathedral. In the Cathedral Museum there is one of Thomas à Beckett's robes, displayed in a glass case. Judging by the size of this garment, we could not help thinking that Thomas must have been a very large man indeed.

Finding a restaurant for dinner was complicated only by the number of excellent choices available. We eventually settled for a small family run business, the Restaurant du Palais located right in front of the cathedral on the Place de la République, where the *prix fixe* menus offered a suitable choice for each of us. After dinner we strolled around the brick-paved pedestrian precinct and made a mental note of several shops that we would want to visit on our way back from Auxerre.

As it turned out, we were able to visit the shops sooner than we had anticipated. Waking up early the next morning to overcast skies and pouring rain, we decided to stay put. We were in no hurry to get to Auxerre and we had here, in Sens, everything that we needed— water, electricity, safe moorings and shops within easy walking distance. Added to this, the port facilities were free as the Port Captain, we found out, was ill, and so he could not collect the port dues. I did make inquiries at the Tourist Information Office about where I could pay the charges, but I only received some rather strange looks in return.

In the afternoon, Antoinette returned from a shopping expedition with two magnificent Dover Sole which she had purchased from the local *poissonnier*. We had them for dinner that night together with our favourite salad of red lettuce, kiwi fruit, pine nuts and Antoinette's salad dressing made from yoghurt, honey and lemon juice.

The next day was again overcast, windy and chilly. It was not exactly the type of weather that makes boating fun. We still had eight locks and sixty-seven kilometres to go before we reached Auxerre, but we had plenty of time in hand before our friends Penny and Sasha Simmons were due to arrive from Bermuda. They were keeping good their promise, made a year earlier in Utrecht, to return for another cruise on the *Bermuda II*.

In addition to the sloping sided locks, we had also heard that the Yonne lock keepers are a breed unto themselves, and this was born out by the events of the following day, by which time the weather had improved considerably.

Arriving at a lock at 11.55 a.m. with the lock gates firmly shut, we observed a man whom we assumed to be the lock keeper, going into his cottage, after having cast a casual glance in our direction. According to my *Carte Guide de Navigation Fluviale* it is customary for the lock keepers on the Yonne to have a half-hour lunch break between 12.00 and 12.30 p.m. We have never begrudged the lock keepers, especially those that operate the manual locks, their lunch break, so we drifted in mid stream taking advantage of the situation to get a quick sandwich ourselves.

After the designated half-hour, the lock keeper had still not returned but I was not unduly concerned. We had all the time in the world— well almost. At 12.50 p.m. there was still no sign of life ashore so I decided to give a honk on our horn to see what response we could get from the lock keeper.

The *Bermuda II* has a klaxon which sounds like a cross between an eighteen wheeler articulated truck and the *Q.E. II*, and a five second blast brought immediate action from on shore. The lock keeper came bounding out of his cottage and with an agitated scowl in our direction he began to crank open the lock gates. Once the gates were open wide, we moved slowly into the lock under the icy stare of the lock keeper. Even my cheery *Bonjour* brought nothing more than a grunt, which in France is most unusual. I sensed that all was not well. I found out all about it, a few moments later, after we were secured alongside the one non-sloping side of the lock. (Yes, just to confuse the innocent boater, some of the Yonne locks have one straight side, and one sloping side.)

The lock keeper closed the downstream gates and opened the upstream paddles to let the water into the lock. Now he had time to deal with this monster on the big blue boat. Advancing towards the *Bermuda II* with murder in his eyes, he came abreast of the stern rail of the boat. He was built like a professional weight lifter. I estimated his age to be somewhere around the late twenties, and he was dressed in dark blue shorts and matching singlet which displayed his muscular sun tanned biceps to great advantage. Striking an aggressive pose, he announced that my manners were less than desirable.

'But, monsieur, what have I done?' I inquired in my best French.

'It was not nice of you to blow your horn while I was having my lunch.'

Grabbing my up-to-date canal Guide, I tried to point out, that it indicated the lunch break was between 12.00 and 12.30 p.m.

'No. The Guide is stupid. It is between 12.00 and 1.00 p.m.,' was the reply. I was also informed that, in any event, it was extremely rude of me to have blown the horn in the first place. Did I not know that he had seen our arrival? I tried to point out that previously I was not absolutely sure that he was, in fact, the lock keeper. This drew a look of complete incredulity. Snatching his battered cap from his head, he pointed to the official Yonne lock keeper's badge. Was I blind? Could I not see that he was indeed the official lock keeper? The official badge was about the size of a bottle top and while my eyesight is reasonable, I defy even 'Dead Eyed Dick' to spot the lock keeper's badge from 200 metres!

I tried to apologize, but this only seemed to add fuel to the fire of his anger. Did I know, he continued, that when I had used my klaxon, it had frightened his wife, his children, his rabbits and his chickens? The latter I was told would probably not lay eggs for at least a month! Finally, I decided to play the same game and went on the offensive. Removing my cap, I pointed to the Royal Yachting Association's symbol, and demanded that he address me as *Capitaine*. I also inquired as to the address of the local navigation authority and the names of his superiors. Much to my complete surprise, this had the desired effect and with a little help from a fellow skipper of a boat that followed us into the lock, we managed to calm him down enough to get him to complete the locking procedure. Passing through the top gates, we bade him farewell and he actually managed a sickly smile.

In actual fact, I was elated, as the entire argument had been carried

Joigny. Half timbered building.

out in French and at long last I felt that I was making progress with the language. Some weeks later, when we returned through the same lock, we gave him a Bermuda key ring, and the resulting broad smile, and relaxed atmosphere, assured us that at last all was forgiven.

Arriving at the ancient town of Joigny, late in the afternoon, we were too tired to explore the town fully that night. We agreed that for now, it would have to be just an overnight stop and we would pay a longer visit on our return from Auxerre. It turned out that we had made the right decision, as in Joigny there are a few fine old timbered buildings predating 1530 when most of the town was destroyed by fire. Narrow medieval cobbled streets also add to the interest of this riverside town and it is well worth more than just an overnight stop.

The next day's cruise up to Auxerre turned out to be a long, tedious process due to the surprising amount of commercial traffic that was coming downstream. At almost every lock, a downstream barge was expected and the locking cycle was against us. Eventually, we arrived in Auxerre where the late afternoon sun created a stunning sight by silhouetting the Cathedral of St. Étienne with an almost peach coloured glow.

We were made to feel very welcome at the Port de Plaisance and after securing the boat alongside, and connecting up to the shore power supply, we sat on the aft deck and enjoyed a well earned drink. Our surroundings were idyllic and we looked forward to exploring Auxerre over the next few days.

Chapter 17

AUXERRE

June19th/July 1st, 1991

The town of Auxerre was everything that we had hoped that it would be. Steep cobbled streets and ancient half timbered buildings married happily with the more modern buildings that spread up the hillside from the banks of the River Yonne. The town was alive with a vitality that was exciting but not intrusive.

From the riverside port, the skyline was dominated by the Gothic Cathedral of St. Étienne and the 167 foot high stone spire of the church of St. Germain. Years previously, after yet another holiday in a hire boat on the French canals, I had come across a photograph of Auxerre, in Hugh McKnight's book *Cruising French Waterways* and I had said to Antoinette, 'One day I will moor our own boat in exactly the spot from where this picture is taken.' My words had turned into reality.

Until this time, we had planned to spend just a few nights in Auxerre before retracing our route back to the River Seine and its junction with the Canal du Loing. We had anticipated making good use of our guests, Penny and Sasha, by getting them to help us tackle the heavily locked route south on the canals Loing, Briare and Centre. We thought that either Montargis or Briare would be a good place in which to pick them up, but Auxerre was such a perfect spot that we decided to alter our plans and designate Auxerre as the rendezvous point. The railway station was only a short distance away from the pleasure port and a visit to the station and consultation of the timetable, confirmed that our friends would have no trouble at all in travelling from Paris to Auxerre by train.

The generator, which was rapidly becoming the bane of my life, so much so, that we had nicknamed it 'Brutus, had once again ceased to function. As the water heater was electric, the prospect of cruising without being able to take hot showers, except when we were connected to shore power, was intolerable.

The pleasure port was operated by Paul, a Dutchman who had moved to France after marrying his French bride. In addition to running the port, Paul also operated a fleet of very modern Dutch built, Linnsen cruisers that were hired out to holiday makers. Paul's wife, a couturière from Paris, had converted an ex-hire cruiser into a workshop and showroom for her very successful business, which was aptly named *Aquarelle*. The dent that was made in our finances when Antoinette purchased an original silk blouse, from this delightful floating house of couture, was money well spent.

After tackling the generator in the confines of the engine room, I found out that the starter motor would have to be either repaired or reconditioned. I approached Paul with a view to having his mechanic take a look at the situation to see if he could be of some help. The mechanic arrived on board, and after a cursory look at the situation, decided that he could not possibly tackle the job and at the same time continue with his regular maintenance work on the hire fleet. He told me that there was a motor repair shop near the port who could recondition the starter motor. The generator itself weighed about 350 pounds and the starter motor was of course, located at the very rear of the entire thing. I had spent several very uncomfortable hours wriggling around flat on my back trying to solve the starter motor problem without moving everything forward. It was now apparent that the whole generator would have to be moved in order to get at the nuts that held the starter motor in place. I was fortunate enough to press gang two visiting English skippers into giving me a hand to shift Brutus. With two of us in the engine room and the other pulling on a long rope up through the engine hatch, we very quickly shifted the generator into a more workable position. After I had removed the starter motor, I cycled down to the recommended repair shop where the mechanic was very helpful and cheerfully told me that they would have everything fixed in a couple of days. True to their word, not only was the motor fixed on time, but two very obliging mechanics delivered the motor back to the boat, and set about installing it. Once they had installed the motor, and checked that it was operational, they very kindly assisted in getting the generator back into position.

A week after our arrival in Auxerre, we were delighted to see Bruce and Kincey Potter, whom we had met a month or so earlier in Épernay, arrive in their bright yellow, hire cruiser. After they were safely moored alongside our starboard side, we invited them on board and over a bottle of chilled rosé wine, we discussed our travels. Like us, they had by now racked up a considerable number of locks, and as this is the subject that is most widely discussed among inland skippers, we had a lot to talk about.

Bruce had not forgotten that in Épernay, I had coveted their two mountain bikes and suggested that we should go out for dinner that night and discuss a suitable financial arrangement. On the rue Joubert, we had previously discovered an excellent small restaurant La Marée that was run by a husband and wife team and specialized in seafood. Later that evening, we trooped up the hill to La Marée and over bouillabaisse and sea bass, we agreed on the bargain price of $100 U.S. for each bike. Our next problem was deciding how, and where, to pick up the bikes in one month's time. Bruce and Kincey were heading down the Canal du Nivernais where they would link up with the Canal Latéral à la Loire and continue on to their hire boat base at Digoin. After working out our schedules, it became apparent that our paths would cross somewhere around Digoin and the transfer could then take place.

We would also have liked to travel south on the Nivernais as we had heard that this was a very pretty canal, but this was one canal from which the *Bermuda II* was excluded. With a maximum permitted head height of only 2.7 metres and an uncertain depth of less than 1.6 metres in one section it seemed foolish for us to take the chance of getting through. It was not so much the head height that worried me, it was the fact that any slight drop in the water level would leave us rubbing along the bottom with serious damage to the propellers a distinct possibility.

Today had been my lucky day, for not only had the starter motor for the generator been repaired and reinstalled, but I had also entered into an agreement that would eventually give us two, almost new, mountain bikes. I had also had an excellent dinner with two delightful new friends thrown in to the bargain.

The next day we observed the *Iron Lady*, an English built, wide beam, canal cruiser pull into the port. We remembered that we had see this cruiser at anchor somewhere on the Seine above Paris, and that we had both agreed that it seemed to be an ideal craft for long-term canal cruising. Wide, long and low, with an aft wheelhouse she looked extremely well planned and was obviously a 'one off' boat built to the specifications of a knowledgeable owner. This indeed turned out to be the case, and after inviting the owners, Tony and Liz on board our boat for drinks, they returned the favour the following evening. The interior of the *Iron Lady* was just as we had imagined, modern, spacious with ample guest accommodation, just perfect. Tony had designed the boat himself from a very rudimentary set of drawings which he showed us in the large and comfortable lounge area of the boat. The steel hull had been built and fitted out in the south of England, and they had then sailed her across the English Channel to France. Tony still had a medical practice in the U.K. and for the present moment they could get away for only a few weeks at a time of summer cruising. We were sorely tempted to make an offer for the *Iron Lady* and had we planned on being away from Bermuda for more than two years, our discussions might have borne fruit, as Tony already had ideas about building another boat. I would have willingly extended our self-imposed two year exile from Bermuda but Antoinette was not quite so sure.

The next few days were spent putting the finishing touches to all our late spring cleaning, in preparation for our guests' arrival. By Sunday, all was ready and the *Bermuda II* fairly gleamed from stem to stern. All was in readiness right down to a large vase of flowers on the saloon table.

On our visit to the railway station we had carefully consulted the train timetable, and we had worked out that the very earliest that Penny and Sasha could arrive from Paris would be about 4.30 p.m. After lunch, we retired for a brief afternoon siesta, and were caught out by the sudden arrival of a taxi. The cheery salutations of Penny, Sasha and son, Lars, were heard as they excitedly clambered on board. Our well laid plans had taken a nose dive when, unbeknown to us, they had difficulties with their flight out of Bermuda which had been delayed by twelve hours. They had changed their travel arrangements, and instead of flying to France via London, they had flown directly from Boston to Paris.

We were delighted to see Penny and Sasha back on board the *Bermuda II* once again, and we were glad that on this occasion Lars was able to come along and join in the experience. It was after midnight when fatigue and jet lag finally put and end to all our conversation as we anxiously caught up on all the news and gossip from home. Before retiring to his bunk in the forward cabin, Penny made a quick reference to their very first night on board the *Bermuda II* in Muiden.

'Hope you've got that gas alarm fixed Tony,' he said with a wink. 'We don't need to be woken up in the middle of the night this time.'

I started to chuckle, remembering our first night on board when the gas alarm had sounded for no apparent reason and it had taken us both quite some time, crawling around on all fours, before we could stop its high pitched squeal.

After one more day and night in Auxerre, we were on our way back down the Yonne and looking forward to tackling the canals of the Centre on our southbound cruise.

Chapter 18

Auxerre to Plagny
243.4 kilometres, 80 locks

July 2nd/9th, 1991

We retraced our route back to the River Seine with stops at Joigny, Sens and Montereau. With our experience of a few weeks earlier, we now knew where all the good mooring spots were so the uncertainty of deciding where to stop, and when to push on, was eliminated. Once we were on the Canal du Loing, we found that with the additional crew on board, the whole locking process was substantially accelerated.

We arrived in Montargis at 7.30 p.m. after a long hard day, and we were all ravenously hungry. Leaving the boat safely moored at one end of the commercial port, we walked into the town and cast a critical eye over the menus that were displayed outside several restaurants. France is, to me at least, a gastronomic heaven so it was no surprise when we found a restaurant that we could all agree on. Once inside the restaurant, Lars chose, as a starter, an interesting salad which we found out later consisted of sautéd tips of pigs ears, resting on a bed of lettuce and tomatoes. At least that is what we were told and I am yet to decide if we were having our legs pulled! Much to his credit, this unusual dish did not discourage our teenage crew member one little bit, and the entire platter was consumed in a matter of seconds rather than minutes.

Over dinner, we discussed the possibility of being able to take advantage of the extra hands on board and of transitting the entire length of the waterway to its confluence with the River Saône at Chalon-sur-Saône. To do this we would have about eight to nine days.

With the help of David Edwards-May's distance tables we calculated that there were 130 locks and 363 kilometres between Montargis and Chalon-sur-Saône. Allowing for Bastille Day, a public holiday, on July 14th, it might be just possible to take our guests to St. Jean-de-Losne, if we could pass through eighteen locks a day. Penny and Sasha had heard us talk a lot about our adopted 'home' port and they were just as anxious to see the place, as we were anxious to show them.

I knew that it was not the distance so much that would be the problem, but the possibility of being delayed at the locks by the passage of commercial craft.

I think that the idea appealed to Penny's competitive spirit and I knew also that they wanted to help us as much as possible in negotiating such a formidable number of locks that lay between us and the River Saône. We agreed that we would give it a try to see just how far we could get before the constraints of Sasha and Penny's holiday timetable put an end to the challenge.

On the next day our departure time of 10.30 a.m. belied the fact that we had set ourselves a strenuous goal, but Sasha and Antoinette, realizing that there would be little time for grocery shopping *en route*, wisely insisted that we take on more provisions.

It was not surprising, therefore, when our desired target of eighteen locks per day fell short by two locks. Our overnight mooring in the tiny pleasure port at Rogny was only possible once Penny had done some impromptu gardening to remove a few overhanging tree branches to allow our superstructure sufficient clearance alongside in the port. Upon discovering a small restaurant close to the port, the ladies managed to convince us that they deserved to be taken out to dinner, to which Penny and I dutifully agreed.

After dinner, in the gathering dusk, we took a leisurely walk around the seven ancient lock chambers that were once part of the original canal. The chambers, which were opened to navigation in 1642, are now bypassed and preserved as a national monument.

Before our departure the next morning, we were approached by a dusky-skinned gypsy lady who was selling hand woven wicker baskets for 150 francs each. Rather perversely, I left Antoinette, whose oral French needs much practise, to do the bargaining. Standing out of sight, below in the galley, I surreptitiously told her to offer the gypsy 50 francs. Poor Antoinette, who hates haggling for a bargain at any time, was both embarrassed, and relieved, when a price of 100 francs was finally agreed upon. Immediately after leaving the port, and after passing through the first lock, we had to stop briefly alongside a quay while we waited for a downstream convoy of pleasure boats to pass us. It was here, that we were approached by yet another gypsy lady hawking almost identical wicker baskets.

'Only 150 francs,' she said persuasively. 'It's a bargain.'

'Sorry, I've just purchased one,' I said, shaking my head from side to side.

'It's a bargain,' she repeated, clearly not believing me. Diving below to the galley, I produced the pristine evidence.

'Where did you buy that?' she said, eyeing the basket in amazement and disbelief.

'I have just bought it for 50 francs,' I lied.

'What! Who would sell you such a basket for only 50 francs?'

'Somebody over that way,' I said, waving my hand vaguely, in a semicircle, that encompassed half of France.

Muttering to herself, and with a look of grim determination on her face, the gypsy went off in search of the competition who would no doubt, if found, be unfairly accused of extreme price cutting.

With a quick look over my shoulder, I told Penny to release our lines, as I had no desire to become embroiled in the hornets' nest that I had probably stirred up!

After lunch, we passed through the town of Briare where the canal is carried over the River Loire by the beautiful Briare aqueduct that was designed by M. Gustave Eiffel, who was also responsible for the famous Eiffel tower that was built in 1889. We were now on the Canal latéral à la Loire which runs parallel to the River Loire itself and passes through some very beautiful countryside.

Our arrival in Léré at 7.15 p.m. meant that once again we had fallen two short of our self imposed eighteen lock target for the day. Over dinner on the aft deck we resolved that we would get an earlier start the next day.

So it was that the next day, under a burning hot sun, we toiled away from Léré to Plagny. The small pleasure port at Plagny was a welcome sight as we arrived just half an hour before the lock closing time of 7.30 p.m. Despite having extended our cruising day almost to the maximum, we still failed to achieve our desired lock quota, but our distance travelled was an impressive seventy-three kilometres.

Chapter 19

PLAGNY TO DIOU
77.2 KILOMTRES, 15 LOCKS

July 10th, 1992

The day dawned bright and clear, and by 7.30 a.m. the sun was already beginning to hint at the scorcher to come. Moorhens, with their bell-like calls searched busily through the reed beds foraging for food, before the heat of the day would force them to retire to the shade of their hidden nests.

I was anxious to get going, as we still had eighty-three locks and 278 kilometres, between us and St. Jean-de-Losne, where Penny and Sasha had a train to catch to Paris at lunchtime, on the 15th. That left us with just four and a half days to complete the trip. Eighteen locks a day was proving to be a difficult target and I was still hoping that we would not meet up with any commercial traffic which would reduce our progress to a crawl.

Penny always favoured an early start, so while the ladies prepared breakfast, we slipped the lines and headed for Lock 20 (Jaugenay) some thirteen kilometres away. This meant that we could all enjoy breakfast underway, before it was time for 'all hands on deck' for the first locking process of the day.

Shortly after leaving Plagny, we passed the branch canal to the town of Nevers situated on the banks of the river Loire. Sasha gazed longingly at the historic town which is descended from a Gallic city mentioned in Caesar's Commentaries. 'Next year,' I promised, as Nevers disappeared slowly from view less than a kilometre and a half away off the port side.

There was a good towpath running alongside the canal and by mid morning Sasha decided that it was time for some serious exercise. We had still not taken delivery of our promised mountain bikes, so our two ancient bone shakers were put ashore. With Antoinette and Sasha pedalling ahead of the boat to inform the lock keepers of our impending arrival, we made good progress. Lars would hop off the boat as we slid into a lock and by the time we had made fast he would have already cranked one downstream gate closed, while the lock keeper worked on the other gate with a little less enthusiasm.

At noon, we had a very pleasant surprise as an English narrowboat came out of the lock ahead of us. It was our friends, Roy and Audrey aboard the *Rosie*. We had first met Roy and Audrey while wintering in St. Jean-de-Losne in 1990 so an impromptu 'raft up' took place, allowing us to swap gossip about mutual friends and events on the canals. They were very excited as they had just put in a bid, at the local estate office, for a stone barn adjacent to the canal, a few kilometres further downstream. Roy marked the position on our map and told us to be sure to take a look as we passed by. The lock ahead of us was now awaiting our arrival and we were in a hurry, so lingering any longer was out of the question. We said our 'goodbyes' and continued on our way south.

It was in the next section of the canal that we had the good fortune to purchase some excellent wine at a very reasonable price. In France, it is not unusual for the more enterprising lock keepers to supplement their income by selling produce to passing boats. Honey, eggs, vegetables, wine and sometimes even live chickens can be purchased at a price far below that charged in regional shops. In every case the produce is straight from the lock keepers own garden—freshness guaranteed!

For reasons that will become obvious, I cannot reveal the number or the name of the lock. We entered this particular lock and once the lines were secured, we were approached by a young lady who asked if we would like to buy some lettuce. Antoinette, always on the lookout for fresh vegetables, immediately grabbed her wicker shopping basket and went off with the young lady to the garden, at the side of the lock keeper's cottage. While we were being let down in the lock, I noticed that Antoinettte, having completed her business in the garden, had disappeared into a cellar alongside the lock keeper's cottage, accompanied by the young lady.

The lock emptied, and being anxious to continue, I looked around for Antoinette who by this time had reappeared, carrying her basket which was full of lettuce resting on some newspaper. Looking like the proverbial cat that had swallowed the cream, she announced that she needed some more money.

'Goodness! Didn't you take enough for a couple of lettuce?' I demanded.

With a finger vertical across her lips, Antoinette gave me that knowing look that, after thirty years of marriage, one does not argue with. It is that type of look that secretly says, 'All is well, just don't ask any questions'. I am sure that every married man recognizes this look and knows equally well that the best thing to do is just that— shut up!

The vendor of the lettuce, also, had by now reappeared alongside the boat and furtively, she reinforced Antoinette's request.

'Zer lock keeper must not know of zis,' she said, speaking in broken English, and duplicated Antoinette's sign language. Once the boat was out of the lock, Antoinette removed the lettuce, and whisking aside the damp newspaper, revealed four bottles of wine that had been hidden beneath.

In the solitude of the garden, the young lady had asked if Antoinette would be interested in purchasing some wine. *Bermuda II* has never been known for its abstinence in the wine department, and Antoinette knew that our 'cellar' under the galley steps was running low. '*Bien sur,*' replied Antoinette, whereupon the woman produced a key that been hidden in her bosom and tied around her neck with a piece of string.

She had taken Antoinette to the cellar alongside the cottage and with a flourish had unlocked the cellar door. Row upon row of unlabeled wine bottles glinted in the dim light. Both red and white wine were available but there was no way of tasting the quality. Having purchased some wine of drinkable but doubtful vintage and origin, from other lock keepers, including on a couple of occasions wine which should have carried a Government Health Warning or would have been equally at home in the petrol tank of a lawn mower, Antoinette did not go wild with her purchases—just two of each.

We did not get to sample the wine till later that day, but when we did we all agreed that it was probably one of the best wines that we had ever stumbled across in France. Considering that the price paid was a mere 20 francs (£2.00) per bottle, we were intrigued. That night, moored in Diou, we frantically went over the canal map, trying to remember which lock it was that had this remarkable cellar.

Several weeks later, we related this story to friends who ran a business in France, and who knew a lot more about what goes on in the wine trade than we did. We were told that the quantity of a particular *premier cru*, in some good years, is often surpassed, and that any surplus over the maximum yield declared for each area by the AOC (Appellation d'Origine Controlée) must be sold for distilling or for vinegar production. This would be akin to asking an Englishman to pour good Brown Ale down the drain. Always looking for ways to engage in the national pastime of diddling the government out of taxes, the enterprising locals bottle the wine and sell it illegally without a label and without the foil capsule which indicates that tax has been paid. It was also suggested that the lock keeper would have been a temporary replacement for the regular lock keeper who was not in attendance.

We had arrived at the small town of Diou at 7.10 p.m. after having travelled a very respectable 77.2 kilometres for the day. Our fifteen lock total for the day put us even further behind on our eighteen locks per day target.

Diou has very little to commend it, which is a pity since the town has made the effort to provide an excellent mooring quay with a water point and which nestles under the shade of some lovely mature trees. After a day of 'lock-bashing' the ladies did not feel like preparing a meal on board, as in addition to fatigue, the conditions below in the galley were sauna-like.

We found the only restaurant in town, located an easy five minutes walk away from the boat. Although the meal was over priced and very substandard, Lars ate everything put in front of him, and some of mine into the bargain! Opening and closing lock gates in France is one sure way to work up an appetite and our energetic teenaged crew member had put in a good day's hard work.

When we returned to the boat, it was still hot below decks so we spent a pleasant hour outside on the aft deck, chatting in the balmy warmth of the night air. We were all quite tired and it was shortly before midnight when we all turned in. I remember waking briefly, some time later, and hearing Penny moving about on deck I knew that the forward cabin was apparently still too warm for sleeping comfort. I made a mental note about installing a 24 volt fan for our guests' future comfort, before falling asleep, and enjoying that particular brand of sleep that comes after having had a day of activity, sun, good wine and the company of good friends.

Chapter 20

Diou to St Jean-de-Losne
198.8 kilometres, 68 locks

July 11th/13th, 1991

By now, we were settling into a routine of early morning starts and cruising all day until the 7.30 p.m. lock closing time brought an end to the day's activities.

In our eagerness to get an early morning start from Diou, both Penny and I forgot to take down the aft flag pole, which, much to Antoinette's annoyance, I insisted on putting in place, at the end of each days cruising. I was proud to display our Bermuda flag, as it was a sight not too often seen on the canals of France. Additionally, it had quite often been the catalyst in starting a conversation with complete strangers which enhanced the social side of our lives, so I rigidly stuck to my evening's routine. Passing under the first low bridge, that day, there was a loud 'crack' as the flag pole broke about eighteen inches up from the deck fitting. It was a minor irritation and the pole, having conveniently split on the diagonal, was fairly easy to repair with a couple of screws and some quick setting Araldite.

As we passed through Digoin, after lunch, we looked around for the bright yellow hire cruiser that our American friends, Bruce and Kincey, had hired for their holiday travels in France. After our agreement in Auxerre I was anxious to complete the transaction. We knew that they had to return the boat to the base in Digoin today but there was no sign of either Bruce, Kincey, or the boat. Reluctantly, we continued on our way south, to Génelard, where we found a precarious mooring alongside the grassed bank, and almost directly in front of

Passing through a lock on the Canal du Centre.

the Génelard lock. Our hungry and exhausted crew were delighted to discover, what turned out to be, a very good restaurant less than fifty metres away from the mooring.

In the morning, both the lock keeper and I were anxious that we should move the boat from the lock approach just as soon as possible, as our position would greatly impede any approaching barge that was lining up for the lock entrance. After a visit to the local *boulangerie* for bread and fresh croissants we were soon on our way.

Not long after our departure, a bright yellow hire cruiser appeared travelling towards us. It was Bruce and Kincey, who were heading up the canal towards Digoin. We had somehow managed to get our dates mixed up, and it was today that the boat had to be returned to the hire boat base. Pulling up alongside each other in mid stream, two mountain bikes and $200 in U.S. cash changed hands, and after exchanging addresses, we both continued in opposite directions.

Thanks to our early start in the day, and the fact that all the locks were mechanized, we made splendid progress. By the end of the day, at St. Léger-sur-Dheune, we discovered that we had broken our record by doing thirty-five locks in one day. It was now assured that we could easily reach Chalon-sur-Saône with time to spare. Indeed, we eventually arrived in Chalon, just after lunch, the next day but not before one last little drama.

As we slowly approached the last lock on the Canal du Centre, which would drop us down the final ten metres to the River Saône, the boat was suddenly pushed violently over to the portside and pinned against the approach quay. So great was the force of the current that was pressing us against the quay, that we had to struggle to free *Bermuda II* from this undignified position. Both Penny and I tried different techniques on the wheel and on the throttles, but the boat refused to budge. At one point, Penny even suggested that I go below to check if the propeller shafts were actually turning! After a hasty check in the engine room, where everything seemed normal, I was panic stricken as the thought of loosing both propellers at the same time flashed across my mind. Were two very expensive, and very necessary parts of my boat lying in the mud on the canal bottom? Eventually, the current slackened slightly, and somewhat shaken up by the experience, we made our way into the lock.

The lockside attendant who assisted us with our mooring lines, seemed most unconcerned about the whole event. It was, he informed us rather off handedly, a common occurrence that was caused by the outflow of waste water from the many factories located a short distance upstream from the lock.

After the locking cycle was completed, we made our exit from the lock, and after half a kilometre eased thankfully out to the wide reaches of the River Saône. After all the slow running on the canals, it was a delight to have the engines ticking over at half speed again, as we cruised downstream towards the pleasure port at Chalon-sur-Saône. We were fortunate enough to find a vacant mooring space, in the busy port, and that night we celebrated with a first class meal at the excellent restaurant Le Gourmand, only a short walk from the port.

The next day was Bastille Day, and as the two locks between Chalon-sur-Saône and St. Jean-de-Losne were closed to navigation, any thoughts of making a dash for St. Jean-de-Losne, were out of the question. Instead, we settled for a day of sightseeing and in the evening, we were treated to a spectacular riverside fireworks display as the French celebrated their national holiday.

After a stealthy 6.15 a.m. departure from Chalon-sur-Saône on

Summer moorings at St. Jean-de-Losne.

Monday morning, not to avoid the port dues, as they had been paid in advance, but in consideration of our still slumbering neighbours. We virtually flew up the river, and with only a nominal delay at each of the two locks, we covered the sixty-four kilometres to St. Jean-de-Losne in almost record time.

Our arrival in the Gare d'eau, just after noon was timed to perfection. As good luck would have it, Robert Bond, one of the partners in the H$_2$O company which owns the majority of the pontoon berths in the Gare d'eau, had some business to attend to in Dijon. He agreed to take Sasha, Penny and Lars, to Dijon railway station where they would be just in time to catch their train to Paris. As on their last departure from the *Bermuda II* a year earlier in Utrecht, there was hardly any time for lingering farewells. We had just enough time to confirm the fact that they would return again next year—never any shortage of willing summertime crew—before Robert announced that he was ready to leave. The last we saw of our three friends, that summer, was the sight of them sitting atop their roll bags in the back of Robert's battered red Citroën 2CV van, as they disappeared in a plume of gravel dust to Dijon.

Chapter 21

DISASTER AND DELAY

July 16th/26th, 1991

After the departure of our Bermuda guests, we had just one week in which to get everything ready for our next visitors, our friends, Rosemary and Larry, from Canada. If we had been in the charter boat business we would have been doing a roaring trade!

Our friendship with Rosemary, goes back quite a long way as Antoinette and Rosemary had been at the University of Toronto together. From past experience, I knew that once Rosemary arrived, it would be difficult for me to get a word in edgeways, as Antoinette and Rosemary would chat away incessantly for hours. Rosemary was, and still is, a formidable conversationalist and holds strong views on many aspects of life, and the current affairs of the world around us. Many times in the past, the three of us have sat up till the wee small hours, debating many subjects of varying interest. Rosemary and I have always enjoyed a good, verbal, jousting match! However, Rosemary's propensity for never ending conversation was to bring disaster, this time.

The day before our planned departure for Lyon, we had arranged an evening drinks party to which we had invited about twenty friends. We had wanted them to meet Rosemary and Larry, and to use the occasion to bid our friends farewell, as it was our intention to winter the boat somewhere in the south of France. The past winter in St. Jean-de-Losne had convinced us that the combination of snow and living on board a boat to not go together very well. We also felt that it was time to revert to our original cruising plan made a year earlier in Holland. We had completed the 'grand circle' of central France without serious mishap, and I believed that our apprenticeship at inland cruising had been successfully accomplished.

It was the Navigational Guide of the mercurial River Rhône that now took up my bedtime reading. I noticed in the Guide, that unlike the locks on the smaller waterways, all of the Rhône locks were equipped with VHF two way ship to shore radio communication. We had never had any requirement to use the VHF radio that was already installed on the *Bermuda II* before we purchased her, so I conducted a series of tests with other boats in the marina just to make sure that everything was in good working order.

On the morning of the party, Antoinette and Rosemary had left the boat, for a last minute shopping expedition, to purchase both supplies for the trip to Lyon, and snacks for the evening's party. During their absence, I had taken up the engine room hatch cover, which was situated in the middle of the main saloon, and I had proceeded to change the engine oil and replace the oil filters. One filter on the starboard side engine had refused to budge, so leaving the hatch open, I walked up to the office to see if Charles had a sturdier filter wrench that I could borrow.

The ladies returned to the boat, and Antoinette, seeing that the hatch was open, cautioned Rosemary of the danger. No sooner were the words out of Antoinette's mouth than Rosemary turned around and with a scream promptly fell into the engine room. If one were watching a comedy film, it would probably have been such a predictable act that it would have had the audience howling with laughter. This was far from a laughing matter.

By the time I arrived back on the boat, Rosemary had been extricated from the engine room and was in considerable pain and some shock. Patricia Gérard, who was a nurse by profession, was summoned and after one brief examination, she rushed off to telephone for the ambulance. A short time later, with siren wailing the traditional lament, the ambulance drew up alongside the pontoons and disgorged three white coated medics. With considerable care they manhandled Rosemary over the high safety rail of the *Bermuda II* and placed her on a stretcher. Larry accompanied Rosemary in the ambulance to Dijon hospital while Antoinette and I sat dismally on the boat, awaiting the diagnosis.

St. Jean-de-Losne. Showing the Gare d'eau in the foreground, the town, River Saône
and the junction of the Canal de Bourgogne and the River Saône (right hand edge).
(Photo: Charles Gérard.)

It was impossible to cancel the drinks party that evening as boat
people do not have the convenience of telephones readily available on
board, and some guests were coming from several kilometres away. It
was not until 7.30 p.m. with the drinks party in full swing, that
Rosemary was delivered, as walking wounded, back to the boat by
the ambulance crew. In addition to extensive bruising, and shock,
Rosemary had suffered four broken ribs, but was bravely trying to
make the best of things. She tried to be sociable with our guests while
sitting in a *chaise-longue* on the aft deck, but the pain finally overtook
her and she went below, where, with Antoinette's help she was able
to slip uncomfortably into my bed. The bunks, in the forward cabin,
were a little too high off the cabin sole to clamber in and out of with
any degree of comfort, so for the next few days my bed was designated
as the Hospital bed.

Rosemary's unfortunate accident had of course delayed our planned
departure for Lyon, but I figured that after a couple of days convalescing, we would be on our way. However, an unforeseen and strange

turn of fate was about to take place that would extend the convalescing period even longer than I had expected.

The next day, while tidying up the aft deck from the previous night's party, I heard a shout from the shore.

'The barges are barricading the port!' The word spread around the Gare d'eau like a summer bush fire, and sent everyone scrambling for their bikes to go and investigate. Sure enough, half a dozen barges were moored stem to stern across the entrance to both the Gare d'eau, and the entrance to the Canal de Bourgogne. Upon arrival at the scene, I could see Charles Gérard arguing animatedly with a burly barge captain. In the background, a small fleet of confused holiday makers in hire boats were milling around on the river. Not being too adept at handling their floating holiday homes, these weekend admirals were engaging each other with some hair raising nautical manoeuvres, and shouting loudly to each other in a variety of languages.

Overhearing the conversation between Charles and the barge captain, I quickly found out what the unusual action was all about. As a result of the declining freight available for transport by water, the barge captains had taken this action to bring the situation to the attention of the French government. A few television and newspaper reporters were on the scene to record the event and to add to the general confusion. I was singled out from the crowd by one rather rotund female reporter who fired questions at me in French. Did I understand what was going on? Where was I from? What were my feelings on the matter? I replied the best way I could with my limited French vocabulary and expressed both concern for the barge captains and for the innocent people whose holiday was being disrupted. By this time a German-crewed hire boat had successfully rammed a British-crewed boat and the two skippers were jousting with boat hooks. Obviously this would be a holiday to remember!

Charles later told me that this was not the first time such industrial action had occurred. On the previous occasion tempers had run high and a crew member on a private boat had actually been shot at by an irritated bargee when the boat had attempted to squeeze through the barricade.

The next day, when visiting the Maison de la Presse, I was considerably relieved to be greeted with conviviality by the locals. They were impressed by the newspaper article in *Les Dépêches* and my reported diplomacy, in having seen both sides of the argument. The *Bermuda II* is quite a conspicuous vessel, and being rammed in anger, by a 350 tonne *péniche* was not something that I aspired to. I also figured that it would be safe to walk along the towpath at night!

Having made their point on Thursday, the barricading barges continued their obstruction, but on Friday the barricade was opened for just half an hour in the evening, to allow pleasure boats in and out of the Gare d'eau. At 9.00 a.m. on Saturday, the barricade disappeared as quickly as it had been put in place, and not wishing to tempt fate any further, I decided that we would leave the Gare d'eau, regardless of Rosemary's cracked ribs.

By 10.00 a.m. we were heading downstream on the placid brown waters of the River Saône.

Chapter 22

ST. JEAN-DE-LOSNE TO LYON
201 KILOMETRES, 5 LOCKS

July 27th/31st, 1991

By now, the stretch of river between St. Jean-de-Losne and Chalon-sur-Saône, held little mystery for us, as we had cruised each way several times before. With only two locks to pass through, on the way to Chalon, it had become a favourite route for a 'mini' cruise when we had visitors who could be with us for only a short time.

Chalon is an interesting town with much to see and do, and has numerous excellent restaurants into the bargain. No trip to Chalon, would in my opinion, be complete without a visit to the Musée de la Photographie. This museum is dedicated to Nicéphore Nièpce, who was born in Chalon-sur-Saône in 1765 and is credited with the invention of photography. The extensive array of old cameras and projectors is quite remarkable. The museum is housed in the eighteenth-century Hôtel des Messageries, on the banks of the River Saône. I would imagine that a photography enthusiast could quite easily spend a whole day engrossed in the well presented exhibits. In addition to the Cathedral of St. Vincent, which dates from the eleventh century, there are also many other fine historic buildings.

Not surprisingly, the pleasure port, ideally situated within easy walking distance of the town centre, is frequently packed with boats. Not having made a reservation on this trip, we were fortunate in obtaining a prime mooring spot alongside the outer pontoon. Although Rosemary was still in some pain from her broken ribs, she did manage

128

to accompany us to my favourite restaurant Le Gourmand where once again we enjoyed a spectacular meal.

The next day, we did not leave Chalon till mid morning and we cruised leisurely downstream to Tournus, where we arrived at 2.30 p.m. The quay in Tournus set aside for pleasure boats, proved unsuitable for a craft the size of *Bermuda II*, as on our approach to the quay, the skippers of several small boats tied alongside warned us by sign language, that the water depth would be a problem for us. Slightly further downstream, I noticed a restaurant barge moored up alongside a stone quay. There was just enough room for the *Bermuda II* to moor ahead of the barge. The quay was intended for the sole use of the restaurant barge but after consulting the skipper, and offering the bribe of a few Bermuda key rings for the crew, he allowed us to share the quay.

We had previously agreed, that we would spend two nights in Tournus which would allow us time to visit the abbey of St. Philibert, built in the Romanesque style, and dating from the tenth century. It was a blistering hot day and the cool interior of the abbey was a welcome relief from the furnace-like conditions of the surrounding streets. We poked around the dimly lit interior and even went as far as investigating the pitch black crypt, which was a pretty useless thing to do as one could not see anything, and had to walk around with outstretched arms. Antoinette's adventurous spirit has often led me to the strangest places in the four corners of the earth, and this was certainly one of them. The area around the abbey was taken up by numerous interesting tourist shops, but we limited our purchases to a few postcards of the abbey and a bottle of wine for dinner that night.

Antoinette had located a laundromat not far from the boat, and instead of using our small machine, which was fine for the two of us, decided to make use of the onshore facility. While she braved the scorching afternoon sun, with four people's laundry in a roll bag, I retired to the cool of the aft cabin for an afternoon siesta.

After half an hour, I had dozed off and was not very happy to be roused by the sound of a loud fog horn being blown at close quarters from the river. Stumbling up into the saloon, I could see a *péniche*, angled at forty-five degrees on to our mooring position, while the captain did his best to let everyone on the river know that he had a mighty fog horn. He clearly wanted me to move and to relinquish my much prized mooring. Even had I done so, there would not have been enough room for him to get completely alongside the length of quay that we occupied. Grabbing a length of twisted metal pipe from the spare parts locker, I waved it in the air and shouted to him that it was impossible for me to move, as I had the engine in pieces. This was, of course a complete lie but it did the trick and he backed off slowly downstream to the sand and gravel quay which was not only more suitable but, in my opinion, where he should have been in the first place. Cunning rather than 'might is right' paid off on this occasion. My afternoon siesta having been so rudely ruined, I stayed in the saloon and gazed out over the river.

It was a hot, sultry afternoon and the only movement on the river, once the *péniche* had left, was confined to a few irradescent dragonflies and the occasional fish jumping for a snack.

Among the group of pleasure craft that were moored up at the pleasure quay, we had noticed the small wooden Thames motor launch, *The Pilgrim*, that we had seen months before in Sens on the River Yonne. We had not noticed anyone on board as we passed and in the light of the event that was about to take place, it was probably just as well.

A large, white flybridge cruiser, flying the German flag, came churning upriver at considerable speed, creating a wake the size of Pacific rollers. Despite my attempts to flag him down to a slower speed, he continued upriver without slackening his speed and charged past the line of moored pleasure craft. When the wake hit the shore, boats were flung about in all directions, several had their mooring stakes torn out, or their mooring lines snapped, as the boats surged back and forth. *The Pilgrim* was lifted bodily on to the low stone quay and fell back into the water with a dull crunch that was quite audible from 200 metres away. If someone had been on board the boat they could have been seriously injured, all due to this water hooligan. This was, fortunately, an isolated incident, and most of the people that we met in our two years of cruising, were extremely cautious and polite when passing moored craft.

I was still complaining about this water bound autobahn driver, when we set off the next day in hot and hazy weather conditions. At Mâcon, we stopped at the public quay to take on more fresh water and we were assisted by an elderly English gentleman from a nearby live-aboard barge, who told us that the afternoon weather forecast was for rain with thunder showers. Right on cue, after lunch, it started to rain and we all left the aft deck and retreated to the saloon where I could helm the boat from the interior steering position.

By mid afternoon we were passing through Villefranche-sur-Saône, and the weather had deteriorated from light showers to a steady downpour. As thunder rumbled in the distance, we looked around for a suitable overnight mooring. The small port de plaisance was full, and in any event, it looked rather grubby and uninviting, so we eventually decided to moor alongside two rusty and disused, empty gravel barges. The barges were half sunken alongside the river bank, and with a ten metre gap between them and the shore, there was no way that we could have safely gone ashore, even if we had wanted to. Later that evening, Antoinette performed her usual magic in the galley and after an enjoyable dinner we all decided to turn in early hoping that the weather would improve by morning.

The activities of the workmen at the large sand and gravel depot, on the opposite side of the river, had us all awake by 7.30 a.m. and our hopes of better weather had been fulfilled. We had a leisurely breakfast as we watched the comings and goings of the sand barges across the river. With only fifty kilometres to go before we reached Lyon, we were in no pressing hurry, so it was not until mid morning that we cast off from the sunken barges and headed slowly downstream towards Lyon.

Rosemary and Larry had shown considerable interest in the various kinds of water fowl that abundantly inhabit the quieter stretches of the River Saône. Antoinette had produced our illustrated copy of the *Birds of the British Isles and Europe* and as we cruised along, both Rosemary and Larry were busy identifying everything that hopped, walked, swam or flew. I feel that they became a little carried away in their enthusiasm as it would appear that we passed everything from the extinct dodo to the greater pacific pelican!

The pleasant countryside soon gave way to the rather dreary suburbs of Lyon, which being the second largest city in France, cover a considerable area. The city of Lyon encompasses a peninsula between the River Saône and the River Rhône. Our lunchtime arrival allowed more than enough time to cruise right around the city and to travel a short distance upriver on the clear waters of the Rhône before we turned back and headed upstream again on the chocolate brown water of the Saône.

During our circuit of the peninsula we had been anxiously keeping an eye out for a suitable mooring and we were quite disappointed to find that Lyon does not have a pleasure port of any sort. Every craft, travelling the inland waterway route between the English Channel, Germany, Holland and Belgium on the way to the Mediterranean, has to pass through Lyon. It is incomprehensible that the city fathers have not seen fit to create a port de plaisance in this large city. After several possible quays were considered, and rejected, we eventually moored alongside the Quai St. Antoine between the footbridge over the Saône and the Pont Bonaparte.

I was most uneasy about our mooring position as any large city is liable to pose a security threat to unattended craft. I therefore made myself quite unpopular, by decreeing that at least one person was to remain aboard at all times. Our sightseeing of Lyon was therefore carried out in shifts, and our visits to the local restaurants were considerably curtailed. This was a great pity as Lyon has the reputation of being the gastronomic centre of France. It turned out however, that my caution was fully justified.

On our second night in Lyon, I was awakened by Antoinette whispering to me that she was certain that she had heard footsteps on the aft deck above our cabin. Stealthily, I slid out of my bed and in the darkness made my way to the bottom of the two steps that separate the aft accommodation from the main saloon. Peering upwards, I could see a shadowy figure attempting to open the saloon port side door. Whirling around, I grabbed a torch from my bedside table and took my time in thumbing a soft nosed bullet into the chamber of my .22 calibre revolver. This might seem an unnecessary armament to carry on board, but was legally purchased in France and was intended for target shooting which I quite enjoy. Whether or not I would have actually pulled the trigger I don't know. I was angry enough at the intruder to have done so. However, at the first glimmer of light from the torch, he was off like a startled rabbit and after running around the fore deck, he vaulted over the starboard rail. Even before I could open the saloon door, he was on the quay and up the steps to the road in a flash. There was no point in following him, and I did not cherish the idea of parading around the centre of Lyon half naked.

Having heard all the commotion, Rosemary and Larry were now awake and they joined us in the saloon where, once again, I double checked the interior barrel bolts on the doors to ensure that they had not been weakened by the intruder. I had installed these bolts two years previously in addition to the very substantial door locks, in case of just such an event. After a quick inspection of the boat's exterior, I could see that nothing was missing, and after refastening the barrel bolts we all returned to our bunks for a couple of hours of fitful sleep.

Rosemary and Larry left us early the next morning to begin their journey home, via Paris and London. Within an hour of their departure, Antoinette and I cast off to continue our journey south, in search of more hospitable places.

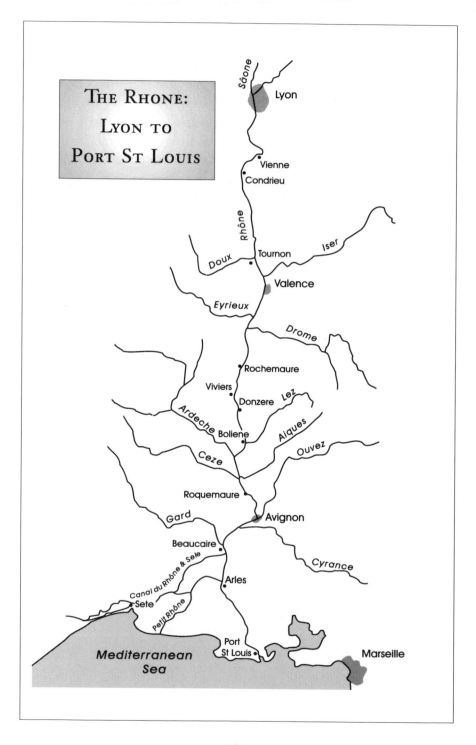

THE RHONE:
LYON TO
PORT ST LOUIS

Chapter 23

LYON TO AVIGNON
250 KILOMETRES, 11 LOCKS

August 2nd/8th, 1991

We left our mooring place just after 10.00 a.m. in typical French summertime weather—sun and lots of it. We headed downstream on the River Saône towards the confluence of the River Saône and the Rhône at La Mulatière. Once again, we were surprised at the contrast between the muddy brown waters of the Saône meeting the crystal clear water of the Rhône at the confluence. This contrast is due in part, to the Rhône having the advantage of originating in the Alps, and due to its shallow draught up until Lyon, no factories looking for cheap water borne transport have been constructed along the path of its winding headwaters. The contrast was as dramatic as it was exciting, for we had read much about the Rhône and we were eagerly looking forward to what lay before us.

The Rhône is a mighty river of ever changing contrasts and the natural beauty of the river valley is breath-taking. When the river is docile, it can have a mesmerising effect, lulling one into a false sense of security. However, the wise skipper will be ever vigilant of the elements that can totally change the whole aspect of the river. Rain or melting snows high up in the catchment area around Lake Geneva in Switzerland can swiftly and dramatically increase the river's current. It is for this reason that no hire boats, other than professionally crewed hotel barges, are allowed on the River Rhône.

When the mistral wind funnels down the length of the valley, it can make life for the unwary pretty uncomfortable. Added to these two

Half way down in a Rhône lock.

factors is the possibility of a southerly wind which can be equally as vicious as the mistral. A combination of mistral and strong current can make travel upstream possible only for those craft with powerful engines. Because of the vagaries of the weather and the distances between suitable stopping places, it is necessary to plan cruises on the Rhône with a little more attention to detail, than one might give, if travelling on other rivers in France.

From Lyon to Port St. Louis at the mouth of the Rhône is a distance of 310 kilometres and with only thirteen locks over the entire distance, a rapid transit is possible for those in a hurry, depending on the direction of travel and the time of year. The locks are huge. They are a minimum of 190 metres long by 12 metres wide, and they vary in height from 9.50 metres to a massive 23 metres, at the Bollene lock. All the locks are equipped with floating bollards which makes locking through comparatively easy.

After just three kilometres of motoring downstream from Lyon, we entered the Pierre Bénite lock which has a fall of 11.80 metres, and we made up astern of the only other occupant of the lock, a large Rhône fuel barge. A commemorative plaque reminded us that this lock was completed and put into service in 1966 and we could not help but wonder what the passage down the Rhône must have been like, prior to its canalization.

Before the locking cycle commenced, the ship's papers were inspected by the navigation authority and our intended destination of Port St. Louis was duly recorded. After being let down in the lock swiftly and smoothly, the large guillotine exit gate rumbled slowly upwards, and once the barge had departed, we cast off from the floating bollards and made our exit into the eleven-kilometre-long uninteresting lock cut, before linking up with the river again at Grigny.

As we passed through the town of Vienne we made a note that at Kilometre Post 29 there was a good public quay, quite close to the centre of the town. We knew that someday we would have to travel back up the river and that a list of suitable stopping places would be useful. We did not stop in Vienne as it was still early in the day and our planned destination for the day was the marina at Les Roches de Condrieu, where according to the navigation map, we would find all facilities.

The wind, which had started out in the morning as just a whisper, had been slowly increasing during the day. By the time we arrived at Condrieu, in the early afternoon, it was blowing a modest 15 knots and increasing. The current on the river, had also increased slightly, presumably due to an increase in the amount of water that was being released by one of the hydro-electric power stations further upstream.

The *Bermuda II* has a canvas 'dodger' that fits around the aft deck, and at slow speeds, and in a cross wind the 'dodger' has a tendency to act as a not very efficient sail. It was inevitable, therefore, that we came alongside the outer pontoon at Condrieu with slightly more of a bump than I would have liked. No damage was done to either the boat or the pontoon as we had taken the precaution of thoroughly fendering the starboard side before making our approach. The port captain quickly took our lines and made us secure. He told us that we had arrived just in time, as the mistral was expected to build up in the afternoon and evening. True to his forecast, the wind increased and other craft, coming alongside in the afternoon, also made more of an arrival than a controlled docking.

Despite the wind, it was still warm and sunny, so we walked around the town above the marina investigating the few small shops. That evening, the mistral flexed its muscles and we knew that if the wind continued, we would have more than just one night in Condrieu.

River Rhône. Les Roches de Condrieu.

The next morning, I did not have to get out of bed in order to see if the wind was still blowing, as the *Bermuda II* tugged strongly at her mooring lines, rocking gently back and forth with each gust. The capitainerie told us that local folk lore has it that the mistral blows for either three, six or nine days at a time, and sometimes continuously for twenty-one days. These multiples of three seem to have no rhyme or reason, and even the local experts cannot predict which of the multiples it will be.

Antoinette tried to take advantage of the stopover by attempting to do a load of laundry in the machine, but the constant movement of the boat threw out the machine's balance mechanism and so she ended up doing everything by hand in the galley sink.

After three days, the mistral blew itself out and the port captain informed us that it would now be safe for us to continue on our way south.

We left Condrieu after breakfast, with not even a wisp of wind to ripple the surface of the river, and headed downstream for our next planned stop which was the Port de l'Épièvre on the outskirts of Valence. We motored very slowly on the broad river which was flanked with rolling grassed hills which slowly gave way to vast areas of vineyards.

The vineyards sported huge signs proclaiming some of the best known names of the producers of the famous Côtes du Rhône wines.

At Kilometre Post 89, we passed the small rock island known as 'La Table du Roi', where St Louis (Louis IX) is reputed to have stopped in his descent of the Rhône, to have lunch on this tiny island. We hoped that the water level was considerably lower at the time of his crusade or else he must have eaten in eccentric solitary confinement.

We passed the small pleasure port at Tournon and for boats slightly smaller than the *Bermuda II* it would appear to be a good stopping place. We could see shops and restaurants immediately opposite to the port which would be extremely convenient for craft in transit.

The vineyards around Tournon were extensive, with hundreds and thousands of vines planted in neat rows which swept down from the hillsides almost to the waters edge. The Crozes Hermitage vineyard alone covers some 1,250 acres, and only on the slopes around the city of Épernay, famous for its champagne production, had we seen such extensive vini-culture.

We arrived in the port of l'Épièvre on the outskirts of Valence, at 3.00 p.m. and we would have been there earlier had it not been necessary to hang around waiting for either upstream, or downstream, commercial traffic at the locks. After one year in France, my French had improved considerably, but I still did not feel confident enough to tackle the lock keepers on the VHF radio. Had I done so, we would probably have been rewarded by such delays being kept to a minimum. This supposition was later borne out on the return trip up the Rhône when I screwed up enough courage to try out the VHF. On more than one occasion that we knew of, it prevented a wait of at least one hour outside a lock.

On entering the port, we found a vacant berth near to the guest pontoon where boats are supposed to wait, pending berthing instructions from the capitainerie. After we were secured, I immediately went ashore and took the ship's papers to the office and reported to the port captain. It turned out that we had by luck, selected a berth that was reserved for visiting craft and so we were spared any further manoeuvring in the confines of the port. The port captain was a very affable young man, and much to my chagrin, wanted to converse in English. As so often happens in France, he was just as anxious to improve his English as I was to improve my French. We finally ended up with him speaking to me in English and my replying in French, an arrangement that was not only fair but had the additional bonus of us both learning new words when we could not grasp each other's meaning.

Although the port is about one and a half kilometres outside of Valence, almost everything that one could ask for is available on site, right down to a good restaurant whose wide verandah offers diners the choice of either dining inside or outside. The evening after our arrival we chose to dine outside on the verandah which has a view overlooking the river and the whole marina. As the evening sun brushed shades of amber and gold on the river, the grey-black cliffs on the opposite shore, briefly turned to deep purple before being enveloped in the gathering dusk.

The next day, we discovered the large Casino supermarket located about 800 metres from the port and we were glad to have our mountain bikes which made the trip relatively easy despite most of the journey having to be made down an extremely busy main road. We also cycled into Valence, although we could have used the bus service which passes the port every hour. In Valence, we visited one of the local banks and cashed a couple of Eurocheques. This process was completed with no problems and afterwards, we then cycled around this very interesting, almost Spanish looking town.

On the following day, we woke up to a beautiful hot, hazy day. By 8.00 a.m. the sailing club's junior members had rigged their dinghies and were all set for a day of sailing instruction on the river. We treated ourselves to a traditional English breakfast with some bacon, from the freezer, that we had bought at Marks and Spencer in Lyon. Together with fresh eggs, tomatoes and a sliced baguette it suitably fortified us for the day ahead. By now, we had adopted the French breakfast habit of croissants and coffee but from time to time the yearning for bacon and eggs could not be overcome.

After Valence, our next planned stop was at the small town of Viviers where the navigation map showed that there was a quay with a water depth of three metres alongside. Upon arrival however, this proved to be totally incorrect, and the one small English sailboat that was alongside was preparing to leave. The skipper told us that the water level had dropped about six inches in the last hour and that his keel was already in contact with the bottom. We considered pushing on further downstream in search of a more suitable mooring. Finally, we decided on a fore and aft mooring arrangement with the propellers held out over deep water by the stern anchor. We were not the only boat to be caught out in this way as several other boats arrived after us and after considering the situation they decided to continue on their way. A small French cruiser was the only exception and they decided to moor up in a similar fashion to ourselves.

We spent a restless night wondering if the water level would fall further which would force us to seek a change of mooring, but we need not have worried. A daybreak inspection revealed that the water level had, if anything, increased slightly. It was another glorious sunrise, but a cloud bank on the southern horizon hinted at rain.

Almost immediately after leaving Viviers we passed through the Donzère gorge, whose dramatic white cliffs on the eastern bank of the river, reminded us of the cliffs of Dover, but on a less extensive scale. We then entered the sixteen kilometre lock cut which leads to the massive Bollène lock, and its accompanying hydroelectric power station. Just three kilometres upstream from the lock, we passed a huge nuclear power station with an interesting contemporary sculpture situated at the water's edge.

The Bollène lock and the hydroelectric power station were, at the time of their completion in 1952, quite remarkable, the lock, with its twenty-six metre fall, the largest in Europe, and the hydroelectric power station producing 10% of France's hydroelectric power. The lock can be filled or emptied in just seven minutes by a series of horizontal sliding sluices in the floor of the lock.

As we approached the lock, the rain which had been threatening all morning, started to pour down, so we donned our foul weather gear and made a rather soggy passage through the lock. Antoinette remarked that the huge guillotine downstream lock gate looked like something out of 'Star Wars'.

Shortly after passing the little town of St. Étienne we cruised by yet another huge power station which was blowing plumes of steam from the cooling towers into the humid air. After the lock at Kilometre Post 214 (Caderousse) the river widened to impressive dimensions. The navigation channel was clearly marked by large stakes on the port side, and where necessary, by buoys on the starboard side. The sun fought a winning battle with the overcast sky and the rain, and so we were treated to views of spectacular scenery. The rolling hills were

One of the many Power Stations along the River Rhône.

dotted with ancient small towns and villages which had been clinging tenaciously to the hillsides for centuries. Castle ruins, and fortified houses were scattered over the landscape, reminding us of the area's tempestuous history. Not only the Romans, but popes, archbishops, dukes and kings had quarrelled and fought over this land for centuries, and today the area is an historian's delight.

By the time that we reached Avignon, the rain had stopped completely and we could see the tourists out in full force on the famous remains of the Pont d'Avignon as we motored slowly past, heading towards the pleasure port.

We were looking through the binoculars for a suitable mooring when a small motorboat with Capitainerie painted in large letters on its side, put out from the shore and made towards us. The capitainerie, after inquiring about our intended length of stay, took up a position ahead of us and guided us into a berth alongside a quay just upstream from the tightly packed pontoons of the pleasure port. He then stood ready on the quayside to take our lines, as we pulled alongside. After making sure that we were secure, he wished us 'Bonjour' and left us alone to tidy up the boat and to put the engines to bed after a very pleasant and interesting cruise down the Rhône.

Chapter 24

AVIGNON AND A CHANGE
OF PLANS

August 1991

The pleasure port in Avignon is ideally situated just a short distance upstream from the famous bridge. The bridge is commonly referred to as the Pont d'Avignon by the English speaking tourists, but more correctly it is in fact the twelfth-century Pont Saint Benezet and with its four remaining arches, it is virtually in the shadow of the walls that enclose this ancient city. The tourist attractions and the main shops are not far away, either by foot or on bicycle.

For the first few days, we played tourists and were quickly disappointed with the advertised attractions. The fourteenth-century Pope's palace, with its crenellated square tower and walls, which added to its military style was a special let down. The vast rooms, stripped of any furniture, were austere and after the first half a dozen rooms they became quite boring. We felt that it was a great pity that this historic building was not presented in a more interesting manner.

Hordes of tourists enjoying the hot sun, swarmed in and around Avignon like ants swarming around a blob of honey. We rigged the awning of the aft deck and this gave us some welcome relief from the relentless sun which had curtailed our activities to late afternoon and evening forays.

After our arrival in Avignon we phoned our son Michael in Bermuda, and we learnt that there was a possibility that he would be attending a technical course in the United Kingdom. We therefore

143

Avignon. The Pope's Palace and the Pont St. Benezet.

decided to remain in Avignon pending the results of his exams, before proceeding the short distance south to the Mediterranean.

From the canal reference books which we carried on board, we knew that theft from boats can be a major problem when moored in the big cities of France. In Paris, at the excellent Port de Plaisance, not only are the entry gates to the basin locked with combination locks at 11.00 p.m. but foot patrols, accompanied by guard dogs, constantly keep a night time vigil over the moored boats. In Lyon, we had successfully scared off a potential burglar thanks to Antoinette being a light sleeper. In Avignon we were not to be so fortunate.

Our two mountain bikes, which we had purchased from Bruce and Kincey, were our pride and joy. Each night while we were in Avignon we had gone through the chore of manhandling the bikes back on to the aft deck of the *Bermuda II*. Returning late one night from dinner on shore, we had not bothered to put the bikes back on board, and had instead chained and locked them to a stout iron fitting that protected the shore supply electricity box. The U-shaped iron pipes were designed to protect the electricity box from being damaged by any cars that might drive along the access quay, and were firmly set in a concrete base. Secured in this fashion, the bikes were less than

144

five metres from the open port hole of the aft cabin and we were sure that they would be quite safe. We should have know better.

At 4.00 a.m. Antoinette woke me with the startling news that she thought that she had heard a slight metallic 'clink' from on shore. In the space of fifteen seconds, I had pulled on a pair of shorts and was standing on the quayside. All that remained of the bikes was the length of chain with the combination lock still attached. The chain had been neatly cut half-way along its length. I was furious, and after having thrown one of our old bikes ashore, and stuffing my revolver into the waist band of my shorts, I set off in pursuit with Antoinette's pleas of 'Take care' still ringing in my ears. In my anger, I must have ridden ten kilometres around Avignon in a futile attempt to locate the thieves. Not a solitary person was to be seen. I was half hoping that at least I would find a gendarme on patrol to whom I could report the theft. It was probably just as well that I didn't, for he might well have taken me into custody. After all, a half naked man with dishevelled hair, riding a battered and unlit bicycle, with a pistol protruding from his waist band at 4.30 a.m. was in itself somewhat of an unusual sight! Frustrated and angry, I returned to the boat where Antoinette consoled me over several cups of hot coffee. In the morning, both the capitain-erie and the local gendarmes were sympathetic but it was, they assured me, all too common a problem in Avignon.

The theft of the mountain bikes did nothing to enhance our feelings about Avignon. When we found out that Michael had passed his exams and would be sent by his company to the United Kingdom, I think that we were looking for any excuse to leave the area, and the boat, for a short time. We quickly made the decision to leave Avignon and to visit Michael in England.

Having made that decision, we were then concerned about where we could leave the boat in comparative safety. Avignon was out of the question, not only due to the events of the past few days, but mainly due to the uncertainty of our return date and the possibility of the Rhône being in flood at the time of our return. We had no experience of suitable moorings in the southern part of France, so we therefore decided that we would take *Bermuda II* back to the only safe place that we knew—St. Jean-de-Losne. Any thoughts of Mediterranean cruising were quickly abandoned.

I estimated that it would take us about a week to make the return trip without working too hard, if of course, the mistral co-operated. So it was that after taking on additional diesel fuel at the quayside pumps in Avignon, we commenced our journey back north.

As we passed through the first lock of the return journey, the slight northerly breeze started to pick up in strength and by the time we reached the wide stretch of river around Roquemaure we were punching into a two to three foot choppy sea. The mistral was already playing its little game with us. The *Bermuda II* took to the slight chop like the thoroughbred that she was, and as the waves increased in size I gleefully watched as the waves broke over the foredeck and sent swirls of water running along the side decks. All too soon, we were back in sheltered waters, and with the bit between her teeth the *Bermuda II* raced north.

Having made notes of suitable mooring places on the way down the Rhône, the rest of our journey was without the uncertainty of searching for overnight stopping places. This greatly increased our daily cruising range and one week later, we were back in the familiar surroundings of St. Jean-de-Losne.

Everyone was surprised and pleased to see us, and over the obligatory glasses of *vin ordinaire* we recounted our adventures many times.

For two days, we worked to prepare the boat for our short absence. We then left St. Jean-de-Losne with the comforting knowledge that the *Bermuda II* was in good hands. Due to a number of reasons, we did not return to the boat until mid September, after which we played host to several groups of visiting friends. Our 'mini cruise', up and down the River Saône to Chalon-sur-Saône was very popular and we got a lot of pleasure out of hosting good friends whose relationship with us went back many years. By the time they had all left, it was almost time to consider the winter. Boats, snow and winter are not the best cocktail in the world we decided, and the offer of a friend's flat in London, together with the fact that Michael would be in England, was just too much to resist. We decided that Christmas and the winter, would be spent in London.

Once again, we left the boat in the capable hands of H_2O in St. Jean-de-Losne, and told Robert and Charles that we would not return until all possibility of snow had passed. It was therefore not until mid March, that we eventually returned to St. Jean-de-Losne and awaited the commencement of the summer cruising season.

Life was never boring on board the boat, and we found ourselves with plenty to do. Antoinette reverted to her profession as a teacher and would spend a few hours each week tutoring Jo-Jo in music theory, in addition to helping me with the interior varnish work. We had never felt so healthy in our lives. Our daily walks, combined with our boat maintenance programme, trimmed a few pounds from our waist lines despite our frequent evening visitations to the Auberge de la Marine where we would enjoy their excellent Bourgogne cuisine. Peter and Germain had spent the winter aboard the *Beulah IV* at M. Blanquart's marina, which was on the other side of the Gare d'eau. The twice weekly music sessions, that were held either on the *Bermuda II* or the *Beulah IV* were a great pleasure to Antoinette and Germain. Mozart himself would have been pleased at the results that were produced on concertina and flute. Now and again, the ladies would use the piano on the *Amicita* but the damp environment created havoc with the piano's ability to stay in tune for any length of time.

One afternoon three small English sailboats, travelling in company arrived in the Gare d'eau. It was not long before we could scarcely believe our ears as the sounds of a string quartet, hard at practice, filled the air. At the first opportunity Antoinette struck up a conversation with the cello player and invited him to join in the following afternoon's music session that was to be held on the *Bermuda II*. These water-borne musicians also had on board an electronic keyboard, the use of which was offered to Germain for the afternoon's session. The only problem was that the keyboard needed a 12 volt supply to operate from, and all our DC electrics on the *Bermuda II* were 24 volt. The keyboard was equipped with a plug that was designed to fit into a car cigarette lighter socket and thus, supply the necessary voltage. After explaining the problem to Charles, he rummaged around and produced the required socket from his supply of secondhand parts. With a spare length of flex, and a couple of alligator clips, we soon had the keyboard operational. Brief musical passages of the afternoon's endeavours were relayed across the Gare d'eau to Peter on board the *Beulah IV*, via VHF radio. This use of the vessel's VHF link, is of course illegal, but being in central France, and using very low power I did, for once, break all the rules. It was a very enjoyable afternoon, and it was a great pity that Timothy, with his cello, could not have remained longer in St. Jean-de-Losne, but the three boats were heading south to warmer climes.

Another weekly entertainment, was the bowling tournament that was held in a small bowling alley on the outskirts of Tavaux which was about ten kilometres away. There were enough cars available among the winter boat residents, to transport fifteen or twenty people over to the bowling alley. Patricia organized the event so that at each gathering the teams were never the same. This was a wonderful way to get to know people that we might only see in passing on the way to the supermarket, or the post office. The bowling evenings were eagerly looked forward to, and the winning team was invariably the one that could cheat in the most imaginative way! It was great fun, and a fierce competition developed between Charles and myself. Our antics of surreptitiously trying to steal each other's favourite ball, or sneaking up behind each other at the moment of delivery, was the cause of much laughter on these light-hearted evenings. I never did manage to achieve a better score than Charles, but that was only because his expertise at cheating was much better than mine!

Having been fascinated by some of Germain's summer pastimes, which included the pickling of walnuts that were gathered from the trees around the Gare d'eau, we were equally impressed by her winter schedule. This included spinning her own wool, making Greeting cards and some projects of greater proportions. They had some friends who owned the château at Longecourt-en-Plaine, where there were many antique chairs with wicker seats, that needed repair. Germain, with her seemingly endless repertoire of talents, re-wove all the seats. While this project was underway the fore cabin on the *Beulah IV* ended up looking like the interior of a weavers cottage and a South American cane forest.

There was in fact, so much to keep us occupied that it was something of a surprise when we suddenly realized that the winter was over and it was time to think about moving on.

Chapter 25

St. Jean-de-Losne to Chalon-sur-Saône

69 kilometres, 2 locks

June 2nd, 1992

The day had finally come. Today was the day when the *Bermuda II* would start the long journey back to her country of origin, and eventually be offered for sale. It was a journey of 1,500 kilometres and we were determined to take our time and enjoy the trip by travelling at a leisurely pace. We knew full well that this would be our final summer of cruising with the *Bermuda II*.

A week earlier, we had announced our date and time of intended departure, so at 9.30 a.m. friends started to gather on the pontoon to say their last minute goodbyes. It was a sad affair as we were not sure when we would see them all again, and we had become a tight knit society sharing our love of boating, France and canal cruising. Our good friends David and Jena looked glumly on as they prepared to give us a hand with the lines to get us out from the tight spot in which we were moored. Patricia had tears in her eyes as we embraced for the last time. We tried to keep things as light and as cheerful as possible but it was proving to be very difficult.

With David pulling on a long stern line to pull us parallel to the line of moored boats that were behind us, we nudged into midstream. With the sounds of klaxons wailing a salute of farewell we headed for the entrance to the Gare d'eau. We passed the barge *Vixit* which had recently been purchased by our friends Mike and Paula who now stood

149

outside the wheelhouse waving goodbye and wishing us good luck. The *Vixit* was the oldest working barge in France at the time of their purchase and they were to have at least a year's work ahead of them converting the barge into a luxurious floating home that would also be suitable for charter.

We passed under the narrow stone bridge that marks the entrance to the Gare d'eau from the River Saône, and motored the short distance to the fuel barge *Avi Saône*. We took on 700 litres of fuel which would easily be enough to see us into Belgium where diesel fuel was considerably cheaper than in France. After bidding farewell to the proprietor Monsieur Burdin, we decided to take one last look at St. Jean-de-Losne from the water, before heading downstream to Chalon-sur-Saône.

We circled slowly under the main road bridge that links the towns of St. Jean-de-Losne on one bank, and the town of Losne on the other. We looked, for the last time, at the sixteenth-century church with its typical Burgundian roof of patterned yellow, black, green and red tiles. A short blast on the horn brought Roy and Audrey to the balcony of their tiny riverside house which they had purchased a year earlier. Roy returned our horn blast by honking away on an old motor vehicle horn of the type with a large rubber bulb on one end.

In a melancholy mood we idled downstream past sights that we had become extremely fond of. Antoinette, sensing my sadness, gave me a comforting hug as I settled back into the helmsman's chair on the aft deck.

It had rained quite heavily overnight, and the sky was still overcast but it was quite warm. The verdant river valley stretched into the distance on both sides of the boat. The white Charollais cattle grazed peacefully in the meadows near the river, and the ever present grey herons rose silently into the air disturbed only by our intrusion into their reclusive world.

We arrived in Chalon-sur-Saône at 4.30 p.m. and much to our surprise and disappointment we found the Port de Plaisance packed with boats. The capitainerie could only scratch his head, shrug his shoulders, and apologize that space was not available for *Bermuda II*. Moving back out on to the river, we managed to find a mooring alongside a wall directly across from the Musée de la Photographie which we had visited on previous trips to Chalon-sur-Saône. The wall was quite high so getting on and off the boat was a little tricky. We cancelled our plans for dinner at one of my favourite restaurants, and opted instead for a meal on board the boat.

The next morning we were up early and after a few housekeeping duties, I clambered up the high wall, and walked over to the Port de Plaisance to see if a space would become available later in the day. After seeking out the port captain who greeted me with a smile and a hand shake, he inquired if we were both well and asked where we were headed. We had been frequent visitors to the port over the past year so he remembered the boat, and our small gifts of a few Bermuda souvenirs which had been well received. After a few more pleasantries, he told me that a few boats would be leaving later in the morning and that it would be a pleasure to reserve a berth on the outer pontoon for the *Bermuda II*.

I thanked him for his consideration, and then spoke to Antoinette on the hand held VHF radio that we had recently acquired. These little devices are inexpensive and are ideal for short range communication. The ones that we had purchased operated within the 'CB' portion of the radio spectrum so no licence is necessary for their use in France. I would thoroughly recommend that anyone who is considering boating through France, equip themselves with this convenient method of short range communication.

Just before lunchtime, we moved into our reserved spot, and then wandered over to the large supermarket that is located just a couple of hundred metres from the port. We had provisioned the boat extensively before leaving St. Jean-de-Losne, but we never tired of exploring the larger supermarkets.

That night, we dined at my favourite restaurant Le Gourmand on the Isle St. Laurent, just a five minute walk from the port. Both the welcome, and the food, were as wonderful as ever, and when we announced that this would be our last visit, Madame insisted that we each had an after dinner liquer on the house. The chef came out from his busy kitchen to wish us *'Bonne chance'* on our journey. We in turn, complimented him on his culinary expertise that we had enjoyed so many times in the past. We decreed that we would return at some future date, whether by car or by boat, in order to enjoy his fine food again. Madame embraced us both as we left the restaurant, and she too wished us a safe and enjoyable journey.

All this farewell business was beginning to get to me, and being somewhat of a romantic at heart, I had a hard job controlling the lump in my throat, on the walk back to the boat.

Chapter 26

Chalon-sur-Saône to Montceau-les-Mines
64.9 kilometres, 44 locks

June 4th/12th, 1992

The next morning, we were on our way by 10.30 a.m. travelling the three kilometres back upstream to the entrance to the Canal du Centre. We waited outside the first lock, while it was being prepared for us, and commented to each other about the rather grim water quality. The water around us was thick, black and oily, evidence of the many large factories just upstream from the lock whose sudden outpouring of waste water had caused us problems when we had been travelling downstream a year earlier. Even the branches of the trees that dipped into the water on either side of the canal were heavily coated with thick black slime. It was the year of the 'Earth Summit' in Rio de Janiero, and Antoinette remarked that the delegates should see this terrible pollution and that they should encourage the French authorities to legislate against this obnoxious situation.

Once we had been brought up in the lock, we received a nice surprise when the lady lock keeper descended from her lofty control cabin and handed us a brochure, in English, giving details about the Central Canal. The cover photograph of a large pleasure boat leaving one of the locks was an immediate indication that on this canal, at least, pleasure boats were welcome. The brochure contained useful information about lock operating times, points of interest along the way, and detailed instructions about the operation of the automatic locks. The brochure was well presented, and I must say that it was the only canal brochure that we ever received on our travels around France. Despite all the well intentioned instructions we were soon to fall foul of the lady lock keeper.

At the third automatic lock upstream, we entered slowly and I poked the bow over to starboard so that Antoinette, who was on the fore deck, could grasp and pull on the dangling blue cord that would close the rear gates, and start the automatic locking cycle. Unfortunately, the ropes had been dangling in the dirty water far too long without replacement. Antoinette therefore had difficulty in discerning which rope was red and which was blue. I was getting exasperated, as I could see Antoinette pulling away at the ropes and yet the rear gates refused to budge. Angrily, I demanded to know what the problem was. Almost tearfully, Antoinette explained that the ropes were about the same colour and when nothing had happened when she had pulled on one, she had pulled the other one as well!

I knew then that we were trapped, and that no amount of pulling on either rope was going to produce a positive result. Apprehensively, I surveyed the high, slimy lock walls and decided that there was nothing to be done other than to scale the equally slimy steel ladder set into the lock wall. Cursing softly under my breath, I cautiously climbed the ladder to see what could be done. There was a small, unmanned control cabin adjacent to the lock chamber and looking through the window I could see a telephone on a plain wooden desk. The door to the control cabin was closed, but not locked as I found out after trying the handle. Upon entering the interior I could see a few numbers scratched into the flaking paint on the wall above the telephone. Not knowing what the numbers were, I decided to try my luck, and dialled the first set of barely legible numbers. For all I knew I could have been dialing the number for the local Pizza express restaurant. A male voice answered on the third ring. I slowly explained the situation that we had unintentionally put ourselves in, and apologised for the fact that we would need some assistance. The voice on the other end of the line became quite agitated and spoke so rapidly that I could only gather that, at that moment, I was not the most popular person in the world. I did manage to grasp however, that something would be done about the situation *tout de suite*. Replacing the receiver, I went outside and gazed over the empty, flat landscape that lay downstream of our elevated position. A cloud of dust appeared on the horizon. As it drew closer, I could make out the shape of a small white car coming along the towpath towards me at high speed.

Our pleasant lady lock keeper was almost beside herself with anger. We were accused of everything from being colour blind to people of uncertain parentage. Apologies were brushed aside with a staccato of French, which left me bewildered and feeling slightly foolish. Finally, the hostility subsided just as quickly as it had started. Madame Éclusiere produced a key and after placing it in an electrical control box, the rear gates slowly began to close.

I carefully made my way back down the slippery ladder and once I had gained the comparative safety of the deck, endeavoured to apologize further to Madame, who was standing on the lockside a good four metres above my head. Due to the acute angle I felt somewhat akin to a turtle whose head would not come all the way out of its shell. My apologies fanned the flames of her anger once again, but on a lesser scale than before. Eventually, her anger gave way to huffy reproach, and then a small smile appeared. All was forgiven.

'For goodness sake Antoinette! Make sure that you get the right bloody one, next time,' I remonstrated. This was very unfair, but poor Antoinette was the only person around that I could now vent my frustration on!

That night, we found moorings in the pleasant little town of Chagny. On the opposite side of the mooring basin, a large hotel barge was a hive of activity and was obviously getting ready to receive guests on board. The crew was busy scrubbing down the decks, while below, we could see the tables being set for dinner. From our vantage point, across the basin, we could also see two chefs hard at work in the galley. We were too far away to see exactly what each chef was preparing but it would sure beat our corned beef hash and salad!

The next day was cold and overcast, and held the distinct possibility of some rain. Before leaving the mooring I made a quick telephone call to Charles Gérard back in St. Jean-de-Losne and requested that he order a couple of impellers for the generator. We were getting less than adequate cooling water through the generator and upon closer investigation, I had discovered that two of the rubber paddles on the impeller had been damaged. Surprisingly, a temporary repair was made

154

by using Super Glue, but I knew that it was just a matter of time before the impeller would once again fail. I told Charles that we would continue up the canal to St-Léger-sur-Dheune, where we would wait for a couple of days for the spares to arrive.

Despite the overcast weather we thoroughly enjoyed our cruise through the unspoilt countryside. We were now far enough above Chalon-sur-Saône to be away from the factories and their terrible pollution. From the canal, we could see the vine-covered slopes around the small town of Santenay which produces an excellent red wine.

At 11.30 a.m. we came to our first lock of the day. The entry gates were open and it appeared that the lock was ready for us to enter. I glanced at the triangular array of navigation lights on the left hand side of the lock entrance, and much to my surprise I noted that neither red, green, nor a combination of either was lit. We had read somewhere, possibly in one of Hugh McKnights books about the French waterways, that if all else failed, waving a frying pan at the radar that controlled the lock, could startle it into operation. *Bermuda II* is a fairly large vessel and this really should not have been necessary, but I was willing to try anything.

Much to Antoinette's amusement, I grabbed a frying pan from the galley and tried a couple of overhead serves. Nothing happened. I tried my forehand—still no result. Even a deadly combination forehand, backhand and overhead smash produced nothing more than giggles from Antoinette, and the confirmation that I looked totally ridiculous standing on the aft deck playing tennis with a frying pan and no ball. A fisherman on the opposite side of the canal with a Gauloise hanging limply from his lower lip, gazed stoically at me and the boat. Retreating under his oversized umbrella he sat on his camping stool making small circles around his temple area with his index finger. I did the same thing back, and indicated that anyone fishing in such a small canal warranted a couple of white coated attendants also. Secretly I hoped that a great white shark would lunge up out of the depths.

I motored into the lock and climbed ashore. Apart from the cars going by on the busy road, not a person was in sight. I flagged down a passing car and asked the driver if he could stop at the next lock upstream, and if there was a lock keeper in attendance, to tell him that we were stuck—once again! The driver readily agreed to do this and after about fifteen minutes, he returned to let us know that the lock keeper was on his way. He got out of the car with his young son, and inspected the *Bermuda II* from stem to stern.

As we were awaiting the lock keeper's arrival I mentally lined up all of my best French excuses in defence of what would surely be another ticking off, for having entered the lock with no indicator lights showing. After a few minutes, the lock keeper arrived and got out of his car. Bracing myself for the onslaught, I decided to attack first.

'The damn lights don't work and the radar is in such a decrepit state that it can't even pick up a boat of this size,' I asserted belligerently. 'Furthermore, this delay has caused me considerable inconvenience,' I continued.

'But Monsieur, I am so sorry,' beamed the lock keeper. 'I can assure you that the lock does work. It's all my fault.' Like a deflated balloon, I stood staring at him hardly able to believe my own ears.

'It is entirely the mistake of the navigation authority. Madame Éclusier, who is in charge of the locks on the first section, told me that you would not be along until tomorrow.' Thrusting a grubby piece of paper under my nose, he indicated a hand written scrawl which clearly said: '*Bermuda II* upstream. 1130 June 6th'.

'Today is the 6th!' I exclaimed.

'Ah! Yes, perhaps you are right,' he agreed, although his puzzled look, and furrowed brow, indicated that he was not quite sure.

'No problem. We all make mistakes.' I took a perverse comfort in knowing that this conversation would eventually be relayed back to Madame who would know exactly what I was getting at. Once again, the 'magic' key appeared and the lock gates closed behind us.

Before leaving the lock, I made quite sure that the lock keeper understood that we would be stopping for a few days in St-Léger-sur-Dheune awaiting parts for the generator. I also informed the lock keeper that we would be in touch with the navigational authority when we were ready to continue on our journey. With a cheery wave, we bade the lock keeper '*Au revoir*' and continued up the canal.

The main claim to fame of St-Léger-sur-Dheune is that it has the lowest canal bridge on the entire central canal system. This is due, in part, to one side of the bridge being lower than the other so that the full head height is not available across the entire width of the canal. We had no difficulty in getting through, but we remembered a year before, when we had passed this way heading downstream. At that time we had seen a large pleasure barge that was having difficulty in passing beneath the bridge. The skipper of the barge, eventually resorted to flooding the bilges in order to lower the barge in the water by a couple of millimetres. Once this was done the barge could just squeeze under the bridge.

The town of St Léger itself, is quite pretty, and has all the essential shops that, combined with a proper pleasure port, makes it an ideal stopping place for boats transitting the canal. There is an excellent *boulangerie* where the bread is baked in the traditional manner in brick ovens, fuelled by wood logs. The bread that we purchased, was among the best that we have ever sampled in France.

We found a mooring just astern of the hotel barge *Papillon* and it was not long before the *capitainerie* came around and almost apologetically charged us 60 francs for a four night stay, which included a charge for the use of electricity.

We were quite happy to wait in St-Léger-sur-Dheune for the generator spares to arrive, and I took the opportunity to have the television set repaired. I was looking forward to watching the satellite TV coverage of the Barcelona Olympics, and the small satellite system that we had purchased a year earlier was proving to be a worthwhile addition to our comforts on board the *Bermuda II*.

On Wednesday, David and Jena drove over from St. Jean-de-Losne with the generator spares. It was good to see them again, and over a welcoming glass of wine, I anxiously asked David if I could take a look at one of the impellers.

'Of course,' said David, producing an impeller from his pocket and placing it on the table.

'What the hell is that?' I said, staring at the extremely large impeller which would have been quite suitable for the Battersea Power Station.

'That's it.'

'For crying out loud! Can't Robert and Charles get anything right? I went all through it with Charles over the telephone. Even down to giving him the number, make and type. That's far too bloody big.'

With a twinkle in his eye, David produced another impeller from his pocket and slid it across the table. 'Then you'd better try this then,' he said craftily.

With considerable relief, I eyed the new impeller and could see that it was exactly right.

'Just winding you up, old son,' said David cheerfully. 'Charles and Robert thought that it would be fun to pull your leg a little.'

I burst out laughing, knowing that those two rascals back in St. Jean-de-Losne would get a good chuckle, when David reported back to them and explained my reaction.

Having got the business, and the joke, out of the way we poured more wine, and caught up on all the local gossip. They left us late in the afternoon, and while Antoinette put one last load of washing in the machine using shore power, I replaced the faulty generator impeller.

The next day, we were up at a reasonable hour and while topping up the water tanks, we watched the red and black hotel barge *Abercrombie* nose into midstream, and slowly head downstream towards Chalon-sur-Saône. The *Papillon* was also planning to leave in a short time, so we said our farewells to Dennis Sherman and his wife before they took on a full compliment of guests, and then they departed, heading in the same direction as the *Abercrombie*.

We made good progress upstream until about midday when we heard thunder rumbling in the distance, and getting closer. Very soon, we were engulfed in a violent summer storm. We waited outside a lock in torrential rain, while the lock keeper struggled with the automatic electrical mechanism. Because of the lightning strikes, the electrical supply was continually being interrupted. The opening and closing of lock gates, became a slow and uncertain business. All afternoon the thunder and lightning continued, and we were reduced to travelling at a snail's pace. If we could have found a suitable mooring, we would have willingly stopped for the remainder of the day, but nothing suitable appeared. The rain continued, and shortly before the designated lock closure time of 7.30 p.m. we were in the small town of Blanzy with no suitable mooring anywhere in sight.

We were wet, cold and exhausted. It had been a terrible afternoon. We searched frantically for a mooring but everywhere at the side of the canal was too shallow. Finally, we could search no further and we reluctantly moored alongside the canal bank and used the roadside crash barrier to pass our mooring lines around. It was not very nautical, and strictly forbidden, but at that point in time all I wanted was to get out of the rain and take a hot shower. Even the thought of food had little appeal. With the boat moored in such a precarious position, bow in and stern out, I knew that we would have to be up before the locks opened at 6.30 a.m. in case of any passing barges.

Getting up early in the morning is not one of my strong points, but I eased myself out from beneath the covers at 5.30 a.m. and put the coffee on. Bleary eyed, and half asleep, I peeked outside to see what sort of a day was dawning. The weather looked promising, and already an early morning sun was starting to burn off a very light mist that hung over the waterway. A quick tap on the barometer glass confirmed that it was on the way up and that we could look forward to an improvement over the previous afternoons atrocious weather.

We arrived in Montceau-les-Mines at 8.20 a.m. having passed through three locks with no delays. At this time of the day we were, for once, the early birds. Montceau-les-Mines has a very small area set aside for pleasure boat moorings, and we were lucky to be able to moor astern of the *Burrus*. They were kind enough to return our favour from St Léger, where we had edged forward to allow them space astern of us and the *Papillon*. With the *Burrus* pulled forward, we were just able to ensure that the stern davits on the *Bermuda II* were not infringing on the navigation channel. We then relaxed over a pot of fresh brewed coffee before investigating our surroundings.

and I were very amused to see that our speculation had been entirely wrong. A handsome young man now escorted her with considerable pride. The elderly gentleman who had seemed to be the bridegroom looked on with fatherly benediction. Photographs were being taken of the bride and groom at various locations around the square. It was not long before two bridesmaids dashed over to where we were moored, and asked if we would object to the wedding party using the boat as a back-drop for a group photograph. We were happy to oblige and a few minutes later the whole wedding party was lined up on the quay alongside the *Bermuda II*.

It was about this time, perhaps fortified with too much wine, that I suggested that a really splendid photograph could be taken if the children from the group were to come on board and line themselves up on the aft deck, with the bride and groom standing below on the quay. This suggestion was met with great excitement, and no sooner were the words out of my mouth, than hordes of children were swarming aboard, over the starboard side of the boat. A great cheer went up from the crowd as the Bermuda flag was hoisted at the stern. Flashbulbs popped away like summer lightning, and I, getting even more into the spirit of the occasion, presented the bride and groom with a selection of Bermuda souvenirs. I had my photograph taken, kissing the bride on both cheeks, and I received a white sugared almond, from a decorated box offered by the groom. I found out later that these sugared almonds are handed out at every wedding in France as symbols of fertility!

The children were by this time into every part of the boat. Antoinette fielded questions from the English speaking members of the wedding party who were eager to practise their English, and left me to deal with the French version of the same questions. What was Bermuda like? What was the population of Bermuda? And, in more than one instance—where exactly was Bermuda? During the question and answer time, the children were still rummaging around the *Bermuda II* from stem to stern. Most of the boys took it in turn to sit in the captain's chair on the aft deck, and by the way that they were wrenching the wheel from side to side, they must have been pretending to navigate around Cape Horn!

Clambering back on to the boat, I made the fatal mistake of showing one young fellow where the horn button was. He promptly set about trying to flatten the batteries! With this unconventional symphony as background music, I set about removing as many young people as I could. I had just about succeeded, when I was approached by a husband and wife holding a tearful little three-year-old girl in their arms. It turned out that the youngster had either been too timid, or too afraid, to get on board the boat, when we had been invaded by the Gallic hordes. Would I mind if the little one came on board to stand on the aft deck? Taking her in my arms, I went up to the aft deck and knelt down, placing her on my knee. We waved to the assembled crowd below, and very soon her tears gave way to delighted giggles as once again, flash bulbs popped from the dockside below. Encouraged by all this attention, she very quickly developed her own version of the royal wave. All went well, until I felt a slight dampness on my right leg. Alas, the excitement had proved too much. Shaking my leg from side to side, I handed her back to her parents. No mention was made of any assistance with the dry cleaning bill!

Before the wedding party left we had our address taken by the father of the bride, who promised that we would receive a copy of the photographs. Sadly, these never materialised as they would have made a nice addition to our photographic journal.

Eventually, everyone returned to their cars and with much honking of horns, waving, and shouts of farewell, they all drove off. We were left alone to reflect on what had been an interesting and eventful day.

Chapter 28

MONTCEAU-LES-MINES
TO DIGOIN
50.2 KILOMETRES, 17 LOCKS

June 14th/17th, 1992

Montceau-Les-Mines is a fair sized town with a population of 27,000, and it is a great pity that there are no real facilities for pleasure boats. Indeed, four small boats would be the maximum number that could get alongside in the area set aside for pleasure boats in the centre of the town. Happily, I understand that this situation is soon to change for the better as plans are afoot to make a Port de Plaisance at one end of the large turning basin, north of Lock 9. With the increasing popularity of the canal, as a holiday cruising area, I am sure that this will pay off handsomely.

We left shortly after 9.30 a.m. after I had strolled over to the lifting bridge to advise the bridge keeper that we would be leaving the mooring basin. Word went out over the navigation authority's VHF radio system that the *Bermuda II* was on the move again.

We had never seen the inside of any central navigation authority office, but by speaking with several lock keepers and other navigation employees the system of 'tracking' the boats was explained to us. In the central office of the respective jurisdictions of the navigation authority there is a large ladder-like board. As a vessel enters the section for which each office is responsible, the name of the vessel is written on a piece of cardboard, which is then slotted into the bottom of the ladder. At the end of the day, the names are re-arranged to indicate the overnight mooring position of each craft within the system. As each vessel leaves one jurisdiction, it is handed on to the next, rather like an Air Traffic controller's board.

As I had taken the time to inform the navigation authority of our intentions that day, all the locks were ready for us. Consequently, we made good time and reached our intended destination of Génelard around lunch time. After topping up with water at the Génelard lock, we asked the lock keeper where we could find a suitable mooring. We were directed to a quay just upstream of the lock where we could see the *Burrus* already moored alongside. It was a lovely sunny, warm day, and being Sunday, I made my regular amateur radio schedule back home to Bermuda. Radio conditions were quite reasonable, and at the first attempt of transmitting 'VP9KG, Victor Poppa Nine Kilo Golf this is F/VP9LR calling, do you copy?' contact was established with our friend Tom Trimingham in Bermuda. As Antoinette listened in to the conversation, we spent a pleasant three-quarters of an hour, exchanging news. We were joined on the frequency by two American friends who were also amateur radio enthusiasts and the resulting four way conversation between Bermuda, France, Massachusetts and Maryland was good fun.

On Tuesday morning, we left Génelard and headed upstream. We were quite surprised at the number of pleasure craft coming downstream, the majority of which were English sailboats of all shapes and sizes, with their masts horizontal over the coachroof, and presumably heading for summer cruising in the Mediterranean.

By 3 p.m. we were in Paray-le-Monial where we took advantage of the tree shaded moorings, to get out of the relentless heat of the sun. Later in the day, when it was cooler, we walked to the famous Basilica of Sacre Coeur, located alongside the River Bourbince. St Hugh, the great Abbot of Cluny, considered that the rural parish church of Paray-le-Monial was too small, and so in 1109 he started building a church on this site. Upon the destruction of the abbey at Cluny, it became one of the few remaining examples of Romanesque and Cluniac architecture. In 1875 the church was elevated to a basilica and is now one of the most important basilicas in all of France. We spent half an hour wandering around the interior that was lit by unexpected shafts of light from cleverly positioned windows which let in the late afternoon sun.

Paray-le-Monial is a useful stop for pleasure craft, although there are no quayside facilities other than refuse disposal. However, as in Monceau-les-Mines, I understand this is soon to change. There was evidence that work had already started on installing quayside electricity supply boxes and, hopefully, fresh water also will be made available. The shopping facilities are excellent and it is well worth one or two nights' stopover to visit this delightful town.

The next day, we set off for Digoin, and *en route* we noticed that the amount of cooling water coming from the starboard engine was not quite what it should be. The temperature gauge confirmed that the engine was running a little warmer than usual. Antoinette took over the wheel while I went below to investigate. I quickly discovered that the rubber hose on the raw water intake was crimping at the place where it made a sharp turn upwards towards the engine block. I was not unduly concerned, as we had spare hoses on board but we did shut down the engine and finished the remainder of the day's trip on just the port engine. We arrived in Digoin around lunch time, and tied up in the Port de Plaisance, where there were both water and electricity available on the pontoons. That afternoon I decided to carry out a little modification to the raw water intake hose on the starboard engine. By fitting a rigid PVC elbow into the rubber hose at the point where it curved upwards towards the engine, I felt that this would eliminate the crimping, and subsequent collapsing of the hose that we had been experiencing. The modification was easy to do, and once the elbow had been secured in place by two hose clamps, we saw that we had a greatly increased water flow from the starboard exhaust.

The Onan generator, continuing to be my *bête noire*, chose this point in time to re-assert its independence. It would start, and then almost immediately, shut down again. I traced the problem to a faulty solenoid. On our walk around Digoin earlier in the afternoon, I had noticed a local garage which displayed an Onan sign on the exterior. I decided to investigate and see if they could be of any help, and so leaving Antoinette on the boat, I walked into town.

The garage was the epitome of a typical country garage where everything from repairs of ploughshares to tractors probably took place. Dirty, dusty, grease stained, cobweb-covered windows added to the rustic, purposeful look of the place. Inside, there was not a car to be seen, only a mechanic wiping off greasy tools with an equally greasy rag.

'*Bonjour, monsieur,*' I announced, clasping the offered greasy hand that was about the size of a leg of mutton. 'Is the *patron* available?'

'But yes, of course, I will get him.'

I was happy to see that now, after two years in France, and having adopted the French habit of shaking hands at every available opportunity, it was finally paying off. To the French, it immediately announces that you are not just another English speaking barbarian.

The *patron* appeared, and after the obligatory handshake, asked in a booming voice befitting his frame, what it was that he could do for me.

I briefly explained the problem with the generator, and that the purpose of my visit was to find out if, at some future point in time, someone could come to the boat to take a look at the generator. Casting an eye around the deserted workshop, I hastened to add that I did not expect anyone to come immediately, nor did I wish them to interrupt their busy work schedule.

'But, of course, I can come right now, this very instant, monsieur,' boomed the *patron*. Waving a magnanimous hand, he indicated a Citroën 2CV van which had seen better days, parked in the forecourt. Producing the keys to this dilapidated vehicle, he invited me to get into the passenger seat. He quickly removed a few odd tools that were littered around on the floor of the van while I removed a mass of chicken feathers, and some left over sacking. Left over from what, I was not quite sure.

I had no sooner seated myself in the van than we took off at an alarming speed. I was still trying to fasten the only seat belt in the vehicle, which just happened to be on my side, when we took the first corner at about 100 kilometres an hour. I surmised that either the local gendarme was on holiday, or that he was related to the driver. Lurching from side to side, we straightened out and hurtled off at breakneck speed towards the port. Arriving on the opposite side of the canal from where the boat was moored, we did an alarming three point turn and flew back in the opposite direction as if we were the local fire brigade which had to get to the boat before it was engulfed in flames.

In a cloud of dust, and a shower of gravel, we pulled up alongside the boat. If anyone had told me that we had taken a wrong turn and had been involved in the French Grand Prix at Le Mans, I might well have believed them. The *patron* disappeared into the bowels of the engine room and after five minutes of poking around, punctuated by numerous '*Ooh, La Las*' and tongue clicking, he announced that what we needed was a 'Cow Chew'. My French had improved considerably over the years, but I had not the foggiest idea what a 'Cow Chew' might be. Declining to stay for explanations, the patron announced that he would return to his garage and come back with a 'Cow Chew' and then we could see what it was that he was talking about. I turned down the invitation to accompany him on the round trip.

After a very short time had elapsed, he returned with the 'Cow Chew' and held it up for our inspection. The 'Cow Chew' turned out to be nothing more than a large rubber ring which, when fitted around the solenoid, kept the plunger in the 'On' position, and prevented the generator from cutting out.

Accepting only a shot of whisky in payment for his services, the *patron* departed and wished us the best of luck on our journey. By using the 'Cow Chew' system, as we now affectionately called it, the generator worked all the way back to Amsterdam, with no further problems. Searching through the French/English dictionary that night we learnt that '*Caoutchouc*' is the French word for rubber!

Chapter 29

DIGOIN TO ST. THIBAULT
157.5 KILOMETRES, 43 LOCKS

June 21st/28th, 1992

Digoin is the point where the Canal du Centre officially ends, and the canal, continuing northwards, becomes the Canal latéral à la Loire. Leaving Digoin behind us, which forever will be remembered by us as 'Cow Chew City', we passed over a 240-metre-long aqueduct, before we reached our first lock of the day. The aqueduct spans the River Loire and offers an excellent vantage point over the surrounding countryside. The river, far below us, seemed to be flowing quite rapidly and our thoughts went back to tales of the barges which, in the seventeenth century, used to make one way passages down the Loire to the sea. The river current was so strong that once the cargo of farm produce and pottery was sold, the barge would be taken apart and the timber sold off. The crew would then walk the 500 kilometres back upstream before repeating the whole procedure once again.

From our experience of the previous year, we knew that the tiny village of Diou offered a good overnight mooring quay, although the depth varied from end to end. Upon arrival, we found that we had the whole quay to ourselves, and by prodding cautiously with the boat hook, we were able to find the exact spot that gave us the greatest depth of water. Having sampled the town's only restaurant on our previous visit, we opted to eat on board that night.

The following day, we found our 'special' lock with the excellent wine cellar. This time, Madame, recognizing the *Bermuda II*, stood with a lettuce in her hand by way of a silent and secret sign, indicating that the cellar was open for business. We stocked up our wine cellar, and promised ourselves that we would reserve a bottle of both red and white wine that was to be enjoyed when our friends Penny and Sasha joined us once again, later in the year. They had very much enjoyed the wine we had purchased the previous year on our way south.

We wanted to visit the town of Decize, and to do this it is necessary to leave the Canal latéral à la Loire, and take a short branch canal through two locks, to the River Loire. It is also possible to continue a short way past the town and to link up with the southern end of the Canal du Nivernais. We passed through the second lock of the short branch canal in company with a hired cruiser and edged into the River Loire. The river, as I had observed earlier when crossing the aqueduct outside of Digoin, was indeed flowing quite swiftly. Once the mooring quay had been spotted, I was grateful for our two 120 hp Ford Lehman engines which easily stemmed the current. Once we had completed our turn, and were pointing back upstream we executed a perfect sideways docking. Meanwhile, the hired cruiser, having spotted the quay at about the same time as we did, tried to turn around in midstream. By the time it had completed the turn, it had been whirled downstream about 500 metres. From that position, and with its engine flat out, it took a good fifteen minutes before it was able to cover the distance back upstream to the quay.

After a two night stay, our departure from Decize, proved to be more of a problem than our arrival. Before we left the quay, I cycled over to the first lock that would take us from the river and back into the canal system. The lock entrance was set almost at right angles to the direction of the river flow. I studied the swirling eddies in front of the lock gates very carefully, mentally formulating a plan of approach. The muddy brown water was churning in a clockwise direction, about ten metres in front of the lock gates. I figured that if we headed for the left hand side of the lock we would be set down just enough to allow us safely to make the centre of the opening. I informed the lock keeper that we would be arriving in about half an hour, and he said that he would have the gates open and ready for us.

I returned to the boat and prepared to cast off. During our departure preparations, we were approached by the French skipper of another boat that was moored up ahead of us. He, too, was concerned about the current on the river and requested that we let the lock keeper know that he would follow us in about an hour. Casting off, we motored upstream and prepared to enter the lock. All seemed to be going well with my prearranged plan, when, at the last second the bow swung violently to port and we headed for the brickwork on the left hand side of the lock. I threw the *Bermuda II* into a brutal reverse that was not guaranteed to do the gear box any good at all, and with blue smoke curling up from the transom, we whirled around for another attempt. On the second time around, everything seemed to be going well until the bow was about two metres into the lock. Suddenly the boat was thrust violently over to starboard. With a sickening sound of steel on stone, the starboard rubbing rail lost about eighteen inches of white paint. The *Bermuda II* bounced off the stone wall of the lock, and under the unperturbed gaze of the lock keeper, she slid the remaining distance into the safety of the lock chamber.

As if to chastise me for my navigational error, the weather promptly turned overcast and it started to rain. For the rest of the day, we continued towards the town of Plagny under heavy skies and intermittent rain showers. We arrived in Plagny by early afternoon, and decided that we had done enough cruising, and damage, for the day. Later in the afternoon, we were joined in the Port de Plaisance, by the French skipper from Decize, who reported that he, too, had great difficulty in negotiating the lock from the Loire. The contest for who had lost the most paint, was declared a dead heat!

Travelling upstream from Plagny the next day, the highlight of our day was in passing the largest field of lavender that we had ever seen. The air was spiked with the delicate aroma of lavender as we cruised by this veritable ocean of purple flowers. The little town of Marseilles lès Aubigny, was certainly one of the saddest looking towns that we had ever passed through. Despite a large, and very modern looking hotel barge that was being built in the central canal basin, the place seemed deserted. Once through the town's two locks, and further on from the hire boat base, a huge factory added to the drab appearance of the place. We hoped that the holiday makers, hiring boats from the base, would not take the immediate surroundings as indicative of what they might expect for the rest of their holiday, for both upstream and downstream there lie interesting and scenically beautiful cruising areas.

We did not reach our intended overnight stopping place of St.

Thibault, due to various delays at the locks, and instead we stopped for the night at a quay in the tiny hamlet of Herry. Long ago, we had learnt that when searching for overnight moorings, the bird-in-the-hand principle was the best one to follow. The mooring at Herry was idyllic. It was the type of mooring that one reads, and dreams about, and if photographed, it would make a wonderful picture postcard. Lofty trees fringed both sides of the canal, and the twittering of the birds was the only sound to be heard in the quiet, wooded setting.

The next morning, we made a leisurely mid morning start, knowing that we had only a short distance to travel to St. Thibault, where we intended to stop for a couple of days. We wanted to explore the town of Sancerre and to sample the well-known wine of the region—hopefully at a reasonable price. After passing through our first lock of the day, we received a pleasant surprise when we saw our friends, Jack and Beth Hanson, whom we had met in St. Jean-de-Losne, aboard their 24 metre barge *Quest*. They were waiting their turn to enter the lock from the opposite direction and were heading downstream towards Decize, and the Canal du Nivernais. Jack listened with interest, to my warning about the state of the current on the River Loire, which they would have to cross to get to the Canal du Nivernais. The *Quest* looked as neat as ever, and unlike us, the reduced head height of the barge made it ideal for cruising on the Nivernais. We did not chat for too long as the lock keeper was waiting, so we said farewell and continued on our way upstream.

Arriving at St. Thibault, we slowly made our way into the embranchment canal where our map indicated that we would find a pleasure port. Much to our dismay, the port was just about full, mainly with permanent live-aboard craft of every description. The few spaces that were vacant had sloping stone walls and were totally unsuitable for us to moor against in safety. We inched our way between the moored craft, and once we had ascertained that we would not find a suitable mooring, we backed slowly astern to the only spot where it was possible to turn the boat around.

As we were completing this manoeuvre, Antoinette remarked that the starboard exhaust seemed to have very little water coming through. 'Here we go again,' I thought to myself, looking over the stern and confirming her observation. I checked below to see if it was the same problem that we had previously, but it was not, the hose looked quite normal to me. We had no alternative but to stop and moor alongside a small craft and investigate further.

Wearily, I turned off the sea cock and removed the nuts from the filter chamber. Apart from the usual collection of duck weed, I could see nothing that was abnormal. Turning on the sea cock with the filter top removed, I expected to be greeted by the normal inrush of water. A trickle of water slid slowly up over the top of the filter chamber and dripped, almost apologetically, into the bilge. I knew then, exactly what the problem was. We had a plastic bag jammed over the raw water intake. I relayed the bad news to Antoinette, and realized that we would have to stay put until we could remove the obstruction.

I tried pushing a long handled scrubbing brush under the hull while clinging on for dear life in the dinghy. This met with limited success and I realized that we only had three viable options. I could go swimming and remove the bag from the outside; we could call on the services of a diver, or I could dismantle the whole filter system down to the sea cock and try to pull the bag through the water intake and into the interior of the hull.

The water quality in the branch canal was revolting. Dead fish floated among a variety of garbage that was strewn across the surface of the stagnant water. I had no goggles suitable for underwater use, so the most economical way out of the situation was to attempt to get at the bag from the inside of the boat. I groaned inwardly when I saw the amount of work that would have to be done in very cramped conditions. Outside, the town of Sancerre beckoned from the hilltop overlooking the river valley, and any decisions would have to wait until the morning.

A short taxi ride took us up the winding road for two kilometres, and soon we were look looking at the view over the valley from the old ramparts. The Loire valley was spread out beneath us in a patch-work of brown and green fields. The vineyards that are responsible for producing the famous Sancerre wine were easily discernible. The vines were in full leaf at this time of year and they were a slightly darker green than the surrounding crops.

We found the town of Sancerre charming, but in danger of losing its innocence to the demands of the tourist trade. Many shops were full of cheap, tacky souvenirs pertaining to the wine industry. Around

The Loire River valley at Sancerre.

the pedestrian precinct, in the centre of the town, every shop seemed to have special 'deals' on Sancerre wine that could be sampled, boxed, and shipped anywhere in the world. Local small cheeses called *crottins* (goat droppings) receive the same treatment and after tasting a small sample, I can confirm, that for my taste at least, the French have the name exactly right! We discovered that the small cobbled side streets away from the areas of most of the tourist activity were the most interesting. Window boxes of bright red geraniums and hanging baskets of colourful flowers graced many of the old buildings, which housed small shops that catered more to the down to earth needs of the locals, than to the tourist trade.

When we returned to the boat, we found a group of people sitting on the grass in front of the small boat which we had moored alongside. We introduced ourselves, and apologized for having to moor in such a fashion and offered to move the *Bermuda II* if necessary. I briefly explained the problem with the cooling system and this was met with much concern and sympathy. The family had just arrived to visit their boat, to air it and to enjoy a glass of wine under the trees. We were invited to join them, so we all sat around discussing the problem with the engine and how best to go about solving it. The family said that they knew an excellent mechanic, and if we wished, they would see if he could come to the boat tomorrow and tackle the job for us. The son was in favour of calling the Nevers Fire Brigade whom, he knew, had a division of experienced scuba divers. I declined both offers and said that I would try to carry out the operation myself, but, if I ran into difficulties I would consider their kind suggestions. I carried a fairly extensive array of tools on board, but there was always the nagging worry of not having the one tool of the right size, for an unusual size nut or bolt. We finished our wine and they departed, wishing us good luck with the repairs and promised to return tomorrow evening to see how we had made out.

In the gathering dusk, we took a stroll around the village and on the way back from the river, we noticed a car with English number plates, pulling into the car park alongside the boat basin. Two men got out of the car and overhearing us converse in English, they introduced themselves as Duncan and Jonathon. They had come to visit friends on one of the moored boats and they asked about the *Bermuda II* which was impossible to ignore in such a small port. Both were sympathetic to our problems, and Duncan, who had some experience with dismantling diesel engines, promised to pay us a visit sometime the next afternoon to see if he could be of any assistance.

I started early the next morning, and climbing into an impossibly small space I started to dismantle the cooling system. The nuts were very difficult to move, paint and time had almost welded them in place. Progress was slowly but surely made however. Finally, with all of the pipes and hoses out of the way I could pass a hooked metal coat hanger through the sea cock. On my first attempt I withdrew about 6 inches of grey plastic bag. Repeated attempts produced more plastic and the water flow gradually increased.

True to his word, Duncan appeared and offered to take over in the cramped confines of the engine room. Duncan toiled away for the rest of the afternoon before he finally announced that the intake was clear and that everything was back in place. I started the engine and we were overjoyed to see a substantial flow of water exiting from the exhaust.

We were very grateful to Duncan for all of his assistance, and we offered to take him and his lady companion, who had arrived earlier in the day, out to dinner that night as a small token of our thanks. He graciously declined the dinner invitation, but suggested that we could buy him a beer or two, at a small riverside cafe, where he was due to meet some friends. After I had cleaned myself up we cycled over to a small rustic shack in a park on the banks of the River Loire. Duncan introduced us to his friends and we all sat sipping ice cold beer under the trees. If it had not been for a couple of noisy jet skis, racing up and down the river disturbing the natural serenity of the place, it would have been perfect.

As usual, when a group of canal enthusiasts gather over a beer, talk turned to tales of the canals. The most amusing story of the afternoon came from Jonathon who told us about the time, a year previously, when he had been on board a sailboat that was making the passage via the inland waterways, from the English Channel to the Mediterranean. He told us that after the first couple of locks on the Canal du Loing, one of the young crew members had offered the lock keeper a cigarette and then rolled another for himself. During the locking cycle, they had stood around puffing on their cigarettes and talking about nothing in particular. The lock keeper became mellow and soporific and after a while gazed soothingly into the mid-distance. In a haze of cigarette smoke, the lock keeper waved them casually on their way at the completion of the locking cycle. From that moment on, all the locks were made ready for them well in advance, and the lock keepers were anxiously requesting a *'Cigarette Anglais s'il vous plait'*. It turned out that the substance being smoked was not your normal everyday tobacco. The lock keepers' two way radio communications system must have worked overtime that day!

Later that evening, our friendly family from the boat alongside which we were moored, came by to see how we were making out. They were delighted when we told them that we had met with success and that the blockage had been removed. They produced two bottles of wine—one to drink now, and one to keep for a later date. With our glasses charged, we drank a toast to France and Bermuda, and to everyone who travels on the French canals. In return for the gift of the bottle of wine, I gave them a selection of Bermuda souvenirs and a mint set of Bermuda stamps that depicted numerous vessels that had been wrecked on the reefs that surround the island. The stamps created

The restaurant 'St. Roch'.

much interest, as it turned out that the father was not only a postman but also an avid stamp collector.

That night, we dined at the restaurant Saint-Roch which is a floating restaurant on the River Loire. It is constructed from two ancient wooden *Berrichon* barges, joined together and converted into an elegant riverside gastronomic paradise. The owner, Madame Arlette Bonlieu, showed us to our table which overlooked the river and produced the extensive menu. The food was excellent! After the events and frustrations of the past few days, we felt that we deserved this treat.

As the evening wore on, a few mosquitoes from the river came flying on board to join us. Anybody looking on from a distance could well be excused for thinking that the diners were carrying on a conversation in semaphore! When we left the restaurant, for the walk to the boat, we were practically eaten alive by some of the largest mosquitoes I have ever seen. We beat a hasty retreat back to the boat, and double checked the insect screening over the port holes. Apart from the drone of the occasional frustrated mosquito, we fell asleep in the peace and quiet of rural France.

motor cycles. (Did I really care to admit to Antoinette that I remembered when every respectable car had running boards?) The extensive collection must have been worth a fortune. A plaque on the exterior of one of the buildings informed us that Napoléon had once spent the night here when the building was an inn. We virtually had the place to ourselves, and we wondered if the dearth of clientele was due to the lack of a sign on the exterior of the premises.

We also dined in the Hôtel du Paris, located adjacent to the pleasure port; the name of the restaurant was more pretentious than the establishment itself. This small, family run restaurant, served us a simple but very good four course meal. The total bill came to 200 francs, which included a litre of the house wine served in an earthernware pitcher. If we had been able to get into the port, I am sure that we would have stayed for at least two weeks! We ended up the evening by sitting around a table with the entire family who owned the restaurant. They were very interested to learn that we came from Bermuda, and questioned us closely about our travels and impressions of France. They were a delightful family and they were excellent ambassadors for this hospitable little town.

After five days in Briare, we decided to leave and to continue on our way northwards to the tiny village of Rogny, where we knew from previous experience that we would find a small pleasure port. We timed our arrival to perfection. As we came through the basin between the last two locks we noticed all sorts of activity taking place on either side of the canal. Directly in front of the ancient, and now disused, seven-lock staircase of the old navigation, scaffolding and floodlights were being erected. Walking into town from the port, we discovered that there was to be a *son et lumière* that night to celebrate 350 years of the opening of the Canal de Briare.

The Canal de Briare is, in fact, one of Europe's oldest canals, having been completed in 1642. The building of the canal was instigated by Henry IV of France, in conjunction with the Duc de Sully, both of them envisaging the advantages of cheap, water-borne freight, between the Seine and the Loire. The king's assassination in 1610 brought an untimely end to the project, and work on the canal did not recommence until 1638, and was finally opened in 1642. The hill at Rogny was the last major obstacle to overcome in linking the Seine river valley with the Loire. Seven lock chambers had to be constructed to allow craft to mount the hill. It is a masterpiece of canal engineering, considering the resources available at that time. The original wooden lock gates have long since vanished but the seven stone-lined lock chambers are now preserved as an ancient monument.

The *son et lumière* was due to start at 10 p.m. so we left the boat at 9 p.m. in order to get a good place alongside the canal basin. Already, throngs of people were lining the bank and looking across to the other side where the technical crew were still putting the finishing touches to the setting. Antoinette, contemplating the length of the spectacle, wisely returned to the boat for two folding chairs so that we could watch in comfort.

The French love fireworks, and virtually any celebration, of any sort, is not complete unless it either starts, or ends, with a display of *feu d'artifice*. Tonight was to be no exception, and shortly after 10 p.m. the show started with a series of Roman candles illuminating the ancient seven locks. The whole town was involved in this stirring, and beautifully costumed extravaganza. We thoroughly enjoyed the event which lasted for about an hour and a half, and ended in another, longer, display of colourful and thunderous fireworks. We returned to the *Bermuda II* at midnight, leaving the locals to continue the festivities at numerous stalls that had been set up to sell wine and beer.

Torrential rain and thunder woke us early the next day, and we remarked to each other it was fortunate that the *son et lumière* had taken place the day before. The rain continued all day so we stayed in the port, happy to just write letters and to laze away the day.

A complete change in the weather the next day, enticed us to continue northwards towards Montargis, where we arrived much earlier than we had anticipated. There was very little traffic on the canal, and the seventeen locks between Rogny and Montargis were negotiated very quickly.

Montargis is known as the 'Venice of the Gatinais' although the metaphor is not one that I would agree with. It is, for sure, a town with numerous small unnavigable canals—but Venice it is not. The section of the canal that cuts through the city, is quite pretty, and is lined on both sides with graceful trees and flower bedecked buildings. To the west of the canal, lies the River Loing which flows into the large Lac des Closiers which offers a wide variety of water sports. Four kilometres north, and just before the entrance to Lock 36 (Buges), is the entrance to the declassified Canal d'Orléans. This canal fell into disuse in 1954, a casualty of not upgrading and enlarging the locks to the Freycinet standard.

We cycled into the town and spent some time browsing around the shops and large department stores. Apart from a few essential groceries, we also purchased a small box of pralines (almond sweets) for which the town is well known.

We decided to leave Montargis after a one night stay, so we cruised north to see what the town of Nemours had to offer. At Nemours, we were once again thwarted by the draught of the *Bermuda II* as the pleasure port had a permissible depth of 1.2 metres only. We did find a good quay, complete with bollards, but this was quite some distance from the centre of the town. As the weather had changed, once again, neither of us felt like cycling into the town in the pouring rain. We decided that any delights that Nemours had to offer would have to wait for another visit, at a later date.

From Nemours it is only twenty-eight kilometres to the confluence of the Canal du Loing and the River Seine. This final section of the canal passes through pleasant countryside, varying between rolling fields and sections of dense forest. The weather was co-operating once again, so it was a pleasant unhurried cruise.

The canal joins the River Seine at the town of St Mammès, which is an important port for the barges that ply the inland waterways of France. As we exited the canal we were quite surprised by the sheer number of barges that were tied up on either side of the waterway. Sadly, the ones that had fallen into disuse out numbered by far, the working barges. With the possible exception of Germany, the amount of cargo being carried through the European canals is steadily declining. We passed row upon row of barges, in various states of neglect. It seemed as if these great behemoths of the inland waterways had come here to die. It was like the legendary and mythical elephants graveyard, where having given up their valuable ivory, the bones were left for the carrion to pick over. Rust streaked and with shattered wheelhouse windows trimmed with flaking brown and black paint, these old barges lay silently together, too old and too tired to move and recapture their past glorious youth. Not a word passed between us as we slid by this woebegone sight.

Turning onto the River Seine, we headed for the fuel quay to exchange one of our used gas cylinders for a new one. We were disappointed to find out that due to recent industrial action by the truck drivers, the depot had not been able to receive replacements. This was not a major problem, as I knew that the cylinder we were currently using, would supply our needs for at least another three weeks. Antoinette took the opportunity to purchase a new pair of heavy duty working gloves from the chandlery shop. This was the fourth pair of gloves that she had worn out since commencing our travels, two years ago. My one member foredeck crew had handled thousands of mooring lines in that period. That night, we found an excellent, but expensive mooring at the pleasure port of Stephané Mallarmé on the River Seine, and on the edge of the forest of Fontainbleu, about two kilometres from the famous château.

It was a comfortable mooring, once the river traffic had ceased at twilight. Later that night, the river became smooth, and as calm as liquid silk. A full moon ascended over the forest of Fontainbleu, and its reflection cast a lattice work of silver over the gentle curve on the river. The calm and serenity of the scene reminded Antoinette of the painting *La charmeuse de serpents* by Henri Rousseau who was inspired by these same forests when he painted his famous work which now hangs in the Musée d'Orsay in Paris.

In contrast to this peaceful night-time scene was our awakening the next day. The first of the river barges started pounding past the mooring at an early hour, moving *Bermuda II* violently in its wake. Antoinette remarked that there was a distinct possibility of succumbing to sea sickness in the aft cabin! Despite the river traffic, we decided to stay where we were, mainly because we had a day in hand before taking up our reservation at the Port de Plaisance, in Paris, but also to do some much needed cleaning of the boat's exterior.

We were up early the following day, and on our way by the unheard of time of 7.20 a.m. I knew that we would be travelling along a busy stretch of the river and I wanted to give ourselves plenty of time in case we ran into any delays at the locks.

At one lock, we were told to enter and to make fast. Having done so, I turned towards the open rear gates and I was horrified to see a large push-tow entering the lock with no fewer than eight dumb barges ahead of it. Seven thousand tonnes of barges, four abreast, slid past our starboard side with just a few centimetres to spare. I recall telling

Sand and gravel Push-Tow on the River Seine.

Antoinette not to worry, as I was sure that it was not the first time that the skipper had carried out such a manoeuvre. I did not share my own conviction as to the skipper's competence. However, the incident passed with no further cause for alarm.

We arrived at the riverside reception pontoon for the Paris Arsenal, at exactly 4.00 p.m. We were delighted to see our friends, Bill and Carol, aboard their boat *The Slow Lane*, waiting patiently at the pontoon before being let into the lock that marks the entrance to the Arsenal basin. We entered the lock together and once the gates had closed behind us, took advantage of the locking cycle to exchange news. Later, we agreed to get together over drinks, and to catch up on a year's worth of cruising yarns.

Once inside the basin we moored at the inside reception pontoon and I went upstairs to the port office and presented the ships papers to the *capitainerie*. After consulting his computer, he gave us the number of our assigned berth, which was at the far end of the basin and almost in the shadow of the monument in the centre of the Place de la Bastille.

The port charges in the Paris Arsenal, are not inexpensive. The rate for *Bermuda II*, which is 14.8 metres overall, was 188 francs per night.

In defence of these charges consideration must be given to the fact that the boats in the port receive twenty-four hour security by guard dog patrols, electricity, and water. Showers, toilet facilities and a coin operated laundromat are also available. Depending on the position of your berth you are never more than 200 metres from the Métro station. Added to this, the Place de la Bastille is virtually in the centre of Paris, so I feel that the charges are justified. Even the smallest of hotels would surely cost more for two people for an overnight stay.

We had timed our arrival to coincide with the French national holiday of Bastille Day. We could think of no better place to be in order to celebrate this, the most important of French holidays. On the eve of Bastille Day, the security patrols were not only patrolling the concourse, but patrols in inflatable boats motored quietly up and down the length of the basin as well. A stray firework, in such a congested mooring place, could have disastrous consequences. The crowds around the Place de la Bastille were full of good humour, and the incessant explosions of fire crackers lasted well into the night. The next morning we were treated to a fly-past by the French air force who flew low right over the port, and the centre of Paris.

We were here to enjoy all of Paris, with its museums, restaurants and places of interest. We planned to stay in the port until our friends Eugene and Sylvia Outerbridge arrived from Canada in two weeks. It was now time to sample the very best of Paris and to visit the places that we had only read about or dreamed of visiting.

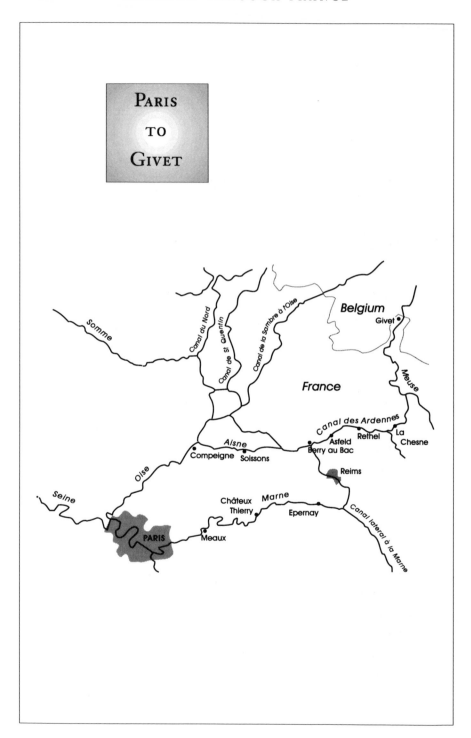

Chapter 31

PARIS TO ATTIGNY
296.4 KILOMETRES, 34 LOCKS

July 31st/August 7th, 1992

The lure of France and a canal cruise had finally enticed our good friends Eugene and Sylvia Outerbridge, away from Eugene's demanding medical career in Montreal. They were to accompany us as far as the France/Belgium border before returning to Canada and a resumption of their busy lives.

Our route would take us down the River Seine to Conflans Ste-Honorine where we would connect with the River Oise. From there we planned to proceed via the Canals lateral à l'Oise, latéral à l'Aisne and the Canal des Ardennes. We would then link up with the River Meuse and travel north towards the French border at Givet.

After leaving the Port de Plaisance, Paris Arsenal, at 9.00 a.m. we turned downstream and joined the convoy of busy river traffic cruising past all the famous sights of Paris. The magnificent Notre Dame cathedral, the Louvre, the Musée d'Orsay and the impressive Eiffel tower. At the lower end of the island known as the Allées des Cygnes, we passed the quarter-scale replica of the Statue of Liberty. The larger, and more well-known version stands in New York harbour and was presented, by the French, to the citizens of the U.S.A. in 1886 as a token of friendship.

It was a hazy, hot day with the temperature of 35°C (90°F) forecast for Paris and its suburbs. It was a delight to be on the water and to enjoy the cool breeze blowing in our faces. The well known Paris tourist boats, the *Bateaux Mouches*, appeared to be doing a thriving business, even at this time of the morning. As each boat passed, the tourists on board would wave and give a quizzical look at our Bermuda flag.

At 4.00 p.m. we arrived at Conflans-Ste-Honorine, and managed to find a suitable mooring by squeezing in between two barges. Conflans is known as 'barge city', and although we had been told this in advance we were none the less impressed by the large number of barges that were moored five and six deep against the quays. Nestled in among them was a 38 metre barge the *Je sers*, which had been converted into a floating chapel. Many of the barges were unladen, and they were waiting for a chance to obtain a cargo from the local freight office, or *Bourse*, as it is known in France. The *Bourse* is rather like a stock market, hence I suppose its name, and the companies offering freight for transport by water, register the details with the *Bourse*. The barge captains register their names, and, on a first come, first served basis, are allowed to bid for the right to convey the cargo. The captains scrutinize a blackboard upon which is written the type of cargo, pick up point, tonnage and delivery point. Bearing in mind all these details, the captain whose name is at the top of the list can either accept, or decline the transportation contract. A rejection by the barge captain still allows his name to remain at the top of the list awaiting a more suitable cargo or destination. Some captains have permanent contracts with various companies so they are spared the daily chore of visiting the *Bourse* to see what freight might be available.

Immediately opposite to our mooring, we found a restaurant which was both reasonable in price and advertised a good menu. After perusing the menu outside the door, Eugene made reservations for 7.30 p.m. We used the rest of the afternoon to explore the town, interspersed with attempts to find a bank with an automatic teller machine that would yield some cash when enticed by Eugene's credit card. Eugene had been assured, back in Canada, that he would find no problem extracting cash with his credit card, from machines throughout France. Sadly, this was not proving to be the case.

The restaurant was as good as its menu promised, and we lingered contentedly over coffee, as the *Bermuda II* bobbed gently at her moorings in plain view across the road.

Early the next morning, Antoinette was standing beside the boat, when she was hailed by a French couple in a passing car. They were on their way to the airport to fly to Bermuda via New York and wondered if the name of our boat had anything to do with their intended destination! There was no time to invite them on board, so Antoinette quickly gave them her father's telephone number in Bermuda, and asked if they would telephone him and let him know that all was well with us. We found out later, that the next day they had paid a visit to my father-in-law at his art studio, in Bermuda. Small world!

We stocked up with some fresh fruit and vegetables from a shop almost next door to the restaurant where we had dinner the previous night and then it was time to leave Conflans-Ste-Honorine.

Casting off our lines, we reversed cautiously into midstream, keeping an eye on the many barges that were passing in both directions, and proceeded a short distance downriver before turning right to the River Oise. The traffic, on the busy River Seine, was immediately left behind, and soon we were cruising through the peace and quiet of the gently rolling countryside of the Oise valley. We passed Auvers sur Oise, where in 1890 Van Gogh had captured *L'église sur Oise* on canvas, and both Antoinette and Sylvia were overjoyed to see the church tower, exactly as Van Gogh had painted it, pass slowly by on the port side. Unfortunately, we could not find a suitable mooring so a trip to the church was reluctantly passed up.

At Creil, we found a good quay alongside a gently rising grassed bank, for our overnight mooring. We were soon joined by the American registered *Bravo* on passage from the English Channel to the Mediterranean. The *Bravo* had damaged her starboard propeller when passing through one of the sloping sided locks on the Canal de la Somme, and the American captain had arranged for a hard hat diver to meet them in Creil to change the propeller. An exercise that proved to be very expensive. I could not help thinking about our encounters with the sloping sided locks of the River Yonne, through which we had travelled a year previously. My caution on the Yonne was well justified, it would seem!

Several months previously, we had arranged to meet our friends Richard and Bronwen Taylor at Compiègne. They would be *en route* to the car ferry at Calais, after a brief holiday, with their daughter Demelza and her friend Claire and they would all be spending the night on board the boat. With the expected multitude of guests the *Bermuda II* would be full to capacity for one night and I guessed that the shower and hot water would be much in demand. We knew from the *Carte Guide de Navigation Fluviale*, that there was a port de plaisance at Compiègne, but we had no knowledge of the facilities that were available there, or if the port would be suitable for a boat the size of *Bermuda II*. We were horrified therefore, to find that the entry to the port was through a very narrow brick archway which just allowed enough room for the boat to squeeze through. The port was only suitable for much smaller craft than ours. By nosing the bow gently into a vacant berth we were able to take on water, but it was obvious that we could not remain with our bow in, and stern out, for the night. Halfway through the water bunkering, we were delighted to hear our friends calling to us from the other side of the chain-link fence that surrounded the port. A quick conversation took place through the fence, as the entry gate to the compound was firmly locked, and we told them that we would finish taking on water and then go back downriver where I had seen a suitable quay, close to the centre of town. It was just as well that we took on the full compliment of 1,200 litres which is the capacity of the boat's water tanks. That night, just as I had suspected, eight people had hot showers before going ashore to search for a restaurant.

My friend, Richard, has visited France many times and he has strong feelings about the type of establishment that he will grace with his patronage for the very serious business of an evening meal. Tonight was no different. Compiègne has a reasonable number of restaurants, and I am sure that we must have read each menu at least twice before Richard finally announced his decision. After all this research one would expect the reward to be an excellent meal, however, this was not to be the case. Although the restaurant was very well appointed, and the staff attentive, the food failed to live up to expectations. Richard's reputation for being able to seek out good eating establishments received a severe blow, along with his pride that night!

After our overnight guests had departed the next day, the water pump decided that it was time for a holiday. After the strenuous exercise of supplying the water for eight showers it was producing only a dribble of water, and that under extreme protest. I decided to tackle the water pump while Antoinette, Sylvia and Eugene went off to visit the Château de Compiègne.

Antoinette later told me that I had missed a very enjoyable experience, as the royal château was extremely interesting. It was built in 1751 by Louis XVI, but was greatly altered later by Napoléon I and Napoléon III. The entry tickets also gave admittance to both the carriage and the bicycle museum where carriages and other forms of transport used by the kings and courtiers of the period could also be seen

Up until recently, one of the best kept secrets of Compiègne is a 900-seat opera house that was commissioned to be built by Napoléon III. The nephew of Napoléon Bonaparte, chose a vacant lot of land adjacent to the palace wall and connected the new building to the palace by an enclosed bridge. As this was intended to be a purely private opera house, a number of apartments were built around it, which to this day still house some of the palace workers. A fund raising project is now under way and, hopefully, sometime in the not too distant future, this interesting relic of the 1870s will be open to the public.

There is another more recent, and less pleasant, historic site a short distance from Compiègne which we did not visit. Eight kilometres away, in a forest clearing, there is a replica of the railway carriage which in World War I served as Marshal Foch's office. On this site, the Armistice to end that war was signed on 11 November 1918. Later, the same carriage was used by Hitler to accept the French capitulation on 14 June 1940 during the Second World War. The original carriage No.2419, was taken to Berlin and was destroyed by fire in the final stages of the war.

Our cruise now took us up to Soissons, and as we approached the town, a few ugly waterside factories reminded us that these canals had originally been built for commercial purpose—not pleasure. Soissons is a city of 32,500 people, and has a rather chequered history. In both World Wars, it suffered tremendous damage as the opposing armies fought for possession of the city. Evidence of the fury of battles, won and lost, can still be seen to this day. Sylvia and Antoinette walked to the Cathedral of St. Gervais and were disappointed to learn that the painting, *Adoration of the Shepherds*, by Rubens which normally hangs there, had been removed for restoration work.

From Soissons, our route took us along the Canal latéral à l'Aisne, which connected us with the Canal des Ardennes at the town of Berry-au-Bac. The Canal des Ardennes is really very beautiful as it cuts through thick forest, where wild boar are reputed to roam, and past remote farms which looked like they had remained the same for centuries. We stopped at Rethel with the intention of just topping up our water tanks before proceeding further, but an infuriating and difficult connection to the oval shaped water tap, delayed us longer than we had anticipated. To add further to our woes, the main water pump on the boat, decided that it had seen enough heavy duty for the time being, and refused to work at all. Eugene and I removed the pump from the engine room where the temperature was above 37°C (104°F) and after stripping the pump down, we found that a faulty diaphragm was the cause of the trouble. Fortunately, we had a spare diaphragm on board, and once Eugene had changed them over, the pump worked perfectly.

It never rains unless it pours, is an old saying, and proved to be true in this case. While we were removing the water pump, I had noticed that we had a small amount of water in the bilge so I switched on the small emergency back-up bilge pump to remove the water. The pump gave a rather sad whine and promptly stopped. Eugene insisted that he be given the opportunity to take the pump apart to see if there was anything he could do to repair it. With considerable patience, befitting a member of his profession, aided by Super Glue and bath-room caulking, Eugene met with success. Once re-installed, the pump worked well and gave us no further problems.

By this time, we had decided to stay in Rethel for the night and to continue on up to Attigny the next day. Rethel turned out to be a pleasant little town, and once the planned port is finished it will make a worthwhile stopping place for boats in transit.

The next evening we were in Attigny, and over a supper of cold meats and salad we planned our assault on the 26 lock flight that lay ahead. Once in the flight, there would be no stopping until we reached Le Chesne at the head of the flight. Our Navigation guide informed us that it would take up to seven hours to complete the flight. An early morning start was planned!

Chapter 32

ATTIGNY TO DINANT
164.4 KILOMETRES, 59 LOCKS

August 8th/14th, 1992

We left the quay at Attigny at 6.30 a.m. sharp, and after passing through two locks we presented ourselves to the lock keeper at the first lock of the Montgon valley flight. We were given explicit instructions by the lock keeper about how to proceed through the staircase. Each lock is electrically operated and the traffic lights at the entrance to each lock are to be strictly obeyed. 'Red' indicates 'stop and wait', 'red and green' shown together means that the lock is being prepared for you, and a 'green' indicates that you may now enter the lock.

There were however, additional obstacles to overcome. At the entrance to each lock there is a hinged, horizontal, metal bar set into the stonework of the lock at water level. This bar has to be pushed forward for five seconds to let the machinery know that you are entering the lock. This system is fine for a barge that takes up the whole width of the lock, but for pleasure boats, with less beam than a barge, it means that a crew member has to push against the lever with a boat hook. Once inside the lock, a vertical, blue metal bar must be pushed upwards to activate and close the rear gates and to commence the filling cycle. A red metal bar, which must be pushed upwards in case of an emergency, would immediately shut down the locking operation, and necessitate the lock keeper riding along the towpath on his motor cycle to investigate the situation. If the red bar is pushed up, it will not only shut down the lock that you are in, but

193

it will also shut down the entire chain of locks, trapping both up-stream and downstream traffic.

Remembering our experience on the Canal du Centre, Antoinette was very careful to make sure that we had our hands on the correct bar! Once the water in the lock has equalized, the exit gates swing open. As the lock is exited, another metal bar, at water level, must be pushed to re-set the lock for the next cycle. In between each lock, there is a very small section, a pound, which allows for the passing of another boat, should one be coming from the opposite direction. In some places, a basin has been dredged at right angles to the canal, but those that we passed seemed to be heavily silted.

All went well in our twenty-six lock climb up the flight, until the penultimate lock where suddenly we could see the lock ahead closing instead of opening. Being the last lock in the chain, a lock keeper was in attendance, operating the lock from his control cabin adjacent to the canal. To our amazement and horror, we saw the upstream gates opening to admit an unladen 350 tonne barge. A sign, immediately alongside our lock indicated that upstream traffic had the right of way. We waited in the lock, expecting the downstream barge to give way and to manoeuvre into the passing basin. No such luck. The barge captain made his way forward to the bow of his barge and exhorted us to vacate the lock. In the meantime, his wife had taken over at the wheel, and the barge was slowly bearing down on us. There was less than 100 metres between the locks, and we were clearly being intimi-dated and were expected to give way and to enter the passing basin. I shouted to the barge captain that I was not happy about entering the basin as it was clearly silted up.

'No. There is enough water for a laden barge.' I was informed, in French.

That being the case, I told him to give way, and indicated the sign.

'*Tant pis* (hard luck). The signs do not apply to commercial craft. Get out of the way,' he shouted back.

The large black barge crept ever closer and a collision seemed imminent. I had no desire to get into a contest that the *Bermuda II* was bound to loose, so reluctantly I pulled over into the basin.

Less than five metres into the basin, *Bermuda II* was firmly stuck in the thick red mud. Our stern was still directly in line with the advancing bow of the barge. However, by gunning the engines, there was just enough room for the barge to clear our aft davits. We looked on anxiously as the barge slid by less than five centimetres away from rearranging the stainless steel davits into some futuristic sculpture. The tension in the air finally dissipated and the crew of *Bermuda II* to a man, rushed below to fortify themselves with a glass of wine, before returning on deck to scowl in unison at the lock keeper who was entirely responsible for the incident.

We entered the last lock of the flight, and shortly afterwards I noticed that the starboard engine temperature gauge was climbing into the danger area. I immediately shut down the engine and asked Eugene to take over the wheel and to proceed on one engine, while I went below to take a look at yet another overheating problem. Undoing the nuts on the main raw water intake, I saw that the filter was packed solid with mud. By opening the sea cock and by back flushing, the blockage was soon cleared and we were able to start the engine and continue on both engines.

At 2.00 p.m. we arrived in Le Chesne and moored up in the welcoming shade of some canalside trees. We had taken seven and a half hours to travel just 16.4 kilometres. This really was the slow way through France! We took the chairs from the aft deck and enjoyed a late lunch and some well earned rest beneath the trees alongside the canal.

Our early morning, Sunday shopping, resulted in a breakfast of fresh croissants, preserves and coffee before we set off at a leisurely pace heading for the end of the canal at Pont-a-Bar where it joins the River Meuse. A sunny day and pleasant countryside made for very enjoyable cruising.

Arriving on the River Meuse was a nostalgic experience for Antoinette and myself, as we realized that in two years we had completed the grand circle of the French waterways. The boundaries of this imaginary circle consisting of the Rivers Seine and Marne in the north, the canals of the Centre in the west, the Canal de la Marne à la Saône in the east and the River Saône in the south. It had been the experience of a lifetime, and we were now heading north towards Holland for the conclusion of our adventure on *Bermuda II*.

The River Meuse seemed to sense our mood and appeared anxious to show itself off in all its glory that day. The ever present grey herons, rose majestically from the gently sloping banks, and overhead, seagulls, far inland from the Dutch coast, wheeled and screeched to each other as they searched our wake for any small fish stirred up by our passage. Weeping willows, lining each bank cascaded their long branches into the water and rustled approvingly at our sedate speed.

The city of Charleville-Mézières soon came into view and we headed for the port de plaisance which we had visited some two years earlier. We were helped into a berth by a friendly Dutch couple who, upon seeing our approach, stood ready to take our bow and stern lines as is the custom among inland waterway travellers. With their assistance we were soon quickly and expertly tied up alongside.

We had decided to have dinner on board that night, and it was just as well that we did. At 6.30 p.m. the sky suddenly darkened and low clouds started to form and scud across a rapidly changing sky. Sylvia, who has studied meteorology, correctly forecast that we were in for a considerable change of weather. We checked our bow and stern lines and put out a couple of springs for good measure. We had no sooner completed our mooring arrangements, when the Port de Plaisance was struck by a mini tornado. Leaves and small branches, torn from the trees by the strong wind, flew through the air. The boat heaved and strained at her lines but with the additional precautions we had taken, we were quite safe. The temperature, in a matter of five minutes, dropped from 30°C (90°F) to 20°C (70°F). After five or ten minutes, the wind dropped as rapidly as it had started and an uneasy calm returned to the port.

We spent two nights in Charleville-Mézières, and probably would have stayed longer had it not been for the fact that Eugene and Sylvia were coming to the end of their holiday. We all enjoyed cruising and we wanted to fit in as much as possible, so we left Charleville-Mézières and continued on our way towards Givet.

At one remote lock, on the way, a young horse came galloping down the hillside, and much to our amazement, stuck his head through the open saloon door and eyed the fruit bowl on the saloon table with obvious interest. Antoinette, who does not like horses at all, and who in fact, is downright scared of them, promptly retreated to the safety of the aft deck. Over the past two years, we had grown accustomed to feeding snacks to lockside dogs, ducks, geese and goats, but this was a first! Eugene gave the horse an apple, which it ate with some speed, and stood expectantly on the lockside, clearly looking for a second helping. This did not materialize, and the horse gazed remorsefully after us, as we made our exit from the lock.

After an overnight stop in Fumay, we arrived in Givet the following day and booked a table at the Restaurant Beaudoin for dinner. This was the restaurant where Antoinette and I had eaten at two years previously on our entry into France, and we were quite surprised when the *maitre d'hôtel* recognized us from our first visit. The meal, and the ambience, were first class, and it was a fitting way to end our French cruising in the company of some very special friends. Next day, Eugene and Sylvia were on their way by 6.30 a.m. and we knew that they would long remember their cruising holiday.

As we were up so early in the morning, we had the whole day ahead of us to catch up on the housekeeping, and all the regular chores. Antoinette located a *blanchisserie* just a short distance from the boat, and this enabled her to get all the sheets and duvet covers washed and dried quickly, ready for our next arrivals.

The *Bermuda II* had always been an hospitable vessel, and both Antoinette and I enjoyed playing host. It was only fitting therefore that the boat should arrive back in Muiden with the same crew that she had left with. Our friends Penny and Sasha had signed up a year ago for the final leg of our journey from Belgium to Muiden and they were due to arrive on August 19th. All that remained was for us to let them know the rendezvous point.

We left Givet in the rain, but by the time we arrived in the Belgian town of Dinant the sun was out and the river was crowded with pleasure boats. We were lucky to find the last available mooring alongside a pontoon just upstream of the main road bridge. The mooring was just far enough away from the noise of the town, yet close enough for it to be only a short distance from the main shopping area. Dinant was preparing for the Assumption Day public holiday, and we arrived just in time to find that the banks were still open which enabled us to change the remainder of our French francs into Belgian francs. We were also able to do some shopping before everything closed down for the weekend. In the town, scaffolding was being erected on the quayside directly in front of the church with its black, onion shaped dome. We later found out that we were fortunate in not being able to get alongside in the centre of the town, as an all night open air disco kept the pleasure boaters awake into the small hours of the morning.

Our mooring was comfortable, and we had water and shore power available on the quayside, so we decided that we would stay and make Dinant the pick-up point for Penny and Sasha. This would allow us a few days in which to clean the boat and at the same time give us an opportunity fully to explore Dinant, as we had spent only one night here on our way south in 1990.

On the Assumption Day public holiday, we discovered that we had unwittingly chosen a ringside seat for the annual bathtub race, or non-mariners boat race. We never did figure out which it was, but the contestants started 500 metres upstream from our mooring, and finished another 500 metres downstream at the main road bridge which spanned the river. We had a grandstand position from where we witnessed some of the most unnautical looking craft that either drifted, or slowly moved past us under power from yet-to-be patented methods of propulsion.

The craft, if one could call them that, ranged from the ridiculous to the extremely clever; there was the bathtub that had been skillfully and beautifully converted into a Viking longboat, complete with squaresail hanging limply from the mast; the floating garden centre; the dog kennel and various other flotsam and jetsam that defied description. The whole object of the 'race' seemed to be to get everyone as wet as possible. Balloons filled with river water were thrown at the boisterous crowds that lined the river bank. The *pompiers*, craftily made use of their tools of trade, and paddled up on the unsuspecting crowd, and then hosed them down with great gouts of water from their converted outside floating toilet. In addition to the various raft-like contraptions, a large pink shark was propelled through the water by the local scuba diving club (how many times could I have used them?). The whole event terminated in a noisy, good natured prize giving that took place on the wharf directly in front of the collegiate church.

On Monday, with the help of the post office, we made an expensive but necessary, telephone call to Sasha and Penny in Bermuda, and gave them instructions about where they could find us in Dinant. We took the rest of the day to acquaint ourselves with some of the tourist attractions which we wanted to visit after Penny and Sasha had arrived.

The shops in the town, were full of the usual mass produced

souvenirs such as ceramic ashtrays featuring a wild Ardennes boar painted in hideous colours, tea towels and other items probably produced in the Far East, and stamped, 'Dinant'. Ardennes ham, sausages and pâté, vacuum packed, and available in every weight, size and shape imaginable, seemed to be a favourite among the German tourists. Street vendors turned out Belgian waffles by the thousands, and neatly stacked them like roofing shingles on their display carts.

Penny and Sasha arrived on Wednesday, and were exhausted after having flown from Bermuda via New York to Brussels. After hungrily devouring some of Antoinette's chicken stew, they retired to the forward cabin to catch up on some much needed sleep.

The next morning, we were all up early and eagerly looked forward to a day of sightseeing. A slight mist still clung to the slopes above the town, but we could already see that we were in for some fine weather. We led Penny and Sasha to the chair lift that rises to the top of Mount Fat. Antoinette is not very keen on chair lifts, but we managed to coax her into joining us. However, after getting her safely to the summit, she vowed that she would walk down, instead of travelling on 'that thing' again! The view from the top was spectacular. The vast panorama of the Meuse valley was spread out beneath us, and one could clearly see why the level land on either side of the main bridge had made this an important river crossing for centuries. On the way down, on foot, a network of galleries, many hundreds of years old, brought us to the prehistoric caves where relics and artefacts from the Paleolithic Age have been found.

In the afternoon, the ladies visited the church of Notre Dame, and reported that apart from its bulbous black spire, it was of no particular distinction. The church was built in the twelfth century and had been damaged, and re-built many times. Later, we decided to visit the Citadel, and faced with either climbing the 400 steps, or taking a cable car to the top, we chose the latter—Antoinette stood in the very middle of the car, and refused to look out of the window. The Citadel is well worth visiting, as this edifice itself is rich in the history of Dinant.

A fortified castle, destroyed by the French in 1703, occupied the original site of the Citadel, and the present fortification was built by the Dutch between 1818 and 1821. The Germans occupied Dinant in 1914 and, during a fierce battle, they torched the city and executed hundreds of Dinant's citizens. The Germans took the Citadel again in

1940; in 1944 it was once more the scene of bitter fighting when the Allies succeeded in liberating the city. Today, it is a museum of military artifacts. It is here also, that the wooden beams of the first Dinant bridge over the River Meuse, built by monks 900 years ago, in more tranquil times, are displayed. Unfortunately, and totally out of character with this historic fortification, the last chamber on the guided tour is a tourist trap. Here, in a Disney-like created bunker, one can have a photograph taken in the sloping room. You can pay at the desk on the way out if you want a copy of this superfluous tourist gimmick.

That night was cause for special celebration as it was Penny and Sasha's 26th wedding anniversary. We ate on the patio of the Restaurant Collegiate overlooking the river. The meal was quite good but unfortunately, not a memorable one. I don't think that we have ever eaten in a restaurant where the waiting staff, out of sheer boredom, ended up playing football, with a large ball of newspaper in the main dining room!

Chapter 33

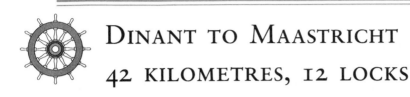

DINANT TO MAASTRICHT
42 KILOMETRES, 12 LOCKS

August 21st/24th, 1992

We were all awake at a reasonable hour in the morning as the first passing barge gently rocked the boat at her mooring. Antoinette and Sasha were the first off the boat as they went to stock up on groceries at the nearby *Match* supermarket. They returned with enough supplies to feed a regiment, and they enthused about the fresh quality of the produce. A packet of Sasha's new found love—Belgian waffles—peeked out from the top of one of the plastic bags.

'Sasha, you're going to gain ten pounds on this trip, if you eat any more of those things,' I teased her.

'You're just jealous,' she retorted good-naturedly and returned to helping Antoinette stow the groceries.

We had only five locks to pass through on our day's cruise to Namur, which would be our overnight stop. We cruised downstream at a gentle pace, through magnificent countryside. I was glad that we had made the decision to pick up our guests in Dinant so that they could enjoy a brief look at the Ardennes scenery. Coming from a small, sub-tropical island like Bermuda, one is always fascinated by sweeping vistas and thick forests. I could see that both Penny and Sasha were delighted by what they saw.

'Heck of a lot of real estate out here,' said Penny appreciatively, as we rounded a bend with not a house in sight. We both smiled and looked at the red rock cliffs, garnished with evergreens, that tumbled down to the water's edge.

five metres up the slope, when all of a sudden, I was surrounded by a veritable army of firemen, police and white coated paramedics who were all dangling from a variety of ropes that were equipped with very professional looking hardware. Very quickly, they strapped the man to a stretcher and hauled him up to the roadway. Surprisingly, I was left to my own devices, and had to struggle back up to the top alone.

On the road was an impressive array of vehicles, and an equally impressive array of manpower. In the stark white lights of the emergency floodlighting, I could see an ambulance, two fire engines, a trailer carrying an inflatable rubber life boat and two police cars. The rotating red, blue and orange strobe lights were attracting an inquisitive crowd.

Once the injured man had been driven away in the ambulance, I looked down at myself. I was covered in blood and grime and festooned with foliage. Antoinette immediately ordered me back to the boat, and outside on the pontoon I was made to strip down to my underpants before being allowed back on the boat. Later, after I had showered and put on clean clothes and was sitting with a large brandy in my hand, the family that Antoinette has asked for help, came on board to thank us for our actions, which I very much appreciated.

On the following day, as we continued downstream heading for Liège, a blood stained rope on the foredeck was a gruesome reminder of the previous night's drama. The crew refused, quite rightly, to have anything to do with this unpleasant souvenir, and despite trailing it overboard, nothing could be done to improve its sinister appearance. I eventually ended up disposing of it, which was a great pity as it was a good length of rope.

As we drew closer to Liège, huge factories flanked both sides of the river. Gone was the beauty of the Ardennes countryside. This dismal industrial architecture, complete with roaring furnaces and high chimney stacks, belched acrid smoke and grime over everything. The river changed colour, tinged by the black and brown sludge that came from the factory outfalls. Towards the centre of Liège, the water quality improved, and impressive modern office buildings, made an uneasy union between old and new, and vied for space overlooking the river.

The Liège pleasure port was completely full, so we had to make do with a mooring on the river side of the protective stone wall which ensures a comfortable night's sleep for those fortunate enough to be moored on the inside. The passing river traffic kept us bouncing around till dusk, but after that things settled down, and we were able to have a peaceful night's sleep after all. The decline in the barge traffic was probably due to the fact that the next day was a Sunday and all inland commercial traffic is forbidden to navigate in Belgium on Sundays. Had I remembered this fact it would have prevented me from cruising up to the Lanaye lock on the Belgium/Holland border, the next day. The lock was closed to navigation and I was annoyed with myself for not remembering this. 'Too long in France,' I said to myself, as we moored alongside the quay that overlooked the small border town of Vise.

Early Monday morning, we were one of the first pleasure boats through the Lanaye lock, and after a brief stop at the Dutch customs, we motored into Maastricht and found a good mooring close to the centre of town. Much to Antoinette's relief, it was also close to several restaurants, which meant that tonight she could negotiate a night off from cooking duties in the galley.

Chapter 34

MAASTRICT TO MUIDEN
335.5 KILOMETRES, 15 LOCKS

August 25th/September 2nd, 1992

It was a blustery windy day, when, after exchanging one of our empty Dutch butane gas cylinders for a new one at the Maastricht fuel barge, we continued on our journey northwards via the Juliana canal. After experiencing the dreary Zuid Willemsvaart canal, two years previously, we had decided to stick as closely as possible to the River Maas which was the only alternative route north, without diverting into Belgium.

The flat countryside of Holland, has considerably fewer locks than France or Belgium, consequently, less delay is experienced in a day's cruising. By mid-afternoon we were tied up alongside the guest pontoon in the extensive Koeweide Yacht Club. We found that a few changes had taken place since our visit of two years previously, in the guise of modernization and profitability. No longer was a nominal charge made for the overnight use of shore power, instead there was a coin operated supply box. Even more objectionable, there was a coin box for the metering of fresh water. There was however, a number of other water taps along the pontoon that could only be turned on by a special key that was presumably available to members only. We had been travelling in Europe far too long not to be equipped with a variety of tools for every occasion, so it was not long before a suitable 'pirate' key was fashioned and our water tanks topped up. I did not feel at all guilty at this subterfuge as we were paying both substantial berthing and electricity rates, and I considered the charge for water to be not only exorbitant but unnecessary.

On the next day, we stopped in Roermond, not only because it was reported to be an interesting town, but also it was the home port of the *Bermuda II* under her previous name of *Cornelia*. On entering the Nautilus Yacht harbour, one of the first sights that greeted us was a smart white glassfibre motor yacht that was flying the German flag, and with the name *Cornelia* emblazoned on the fly-bridge. After securing a mooring, we walked over to the *Cornelia* to see if anyone was on board. Unfortunately, there was no one but we left word with people on the adjacent boat to say that we had stopped by. We spent a pleasant afternoon walking around Roermond with its cobbled streets and little shops, before returning to the boat for a lazy, sociable evening.

Our next overnight stop was Wansuum, where we were lucky to find a vacant berth in the small and congested, pleasure port. The overnight charge of Dfl 19.5 was paid reluctantly on our way out of the port the next day. The port did not include even a water tap amongst its pontoon facilities.

As we made our departure from Wansuum, we were just in time to see the largest craft that we had ever seen on any inland waterway. This ungainly looking craft was a huge push tow with a hydraulically operated wheelhouse that could be lowered automatically when approaching bridges. Ahead of the wheelhouse was a dumb barge about the size of a football field. It was not a pretty sight, but I would imagine that it was highly cost effective for moving the large cargo of scrap metal from one place to another.

At Sambeek, we were packed into the lock like sardines, with only a few inches of space between each craft. The warning siren, advising that the locking cycle had commenced, had already been sounded when suddenly, another siren blast indicated that the process was being reversed. Anxious skippers looked around the lock and at each craft, trying to find out the reason for this unusual procedure. Once the water level had equalized, the lock gates astern of us re-opened and a Water Police boat rapidly entered the lock after turfing out the pleasure craft that was nearest to the rear gates. During the locking cycle, one of the Water Police walked the length of the lock and had a word with the skipper of each boat that was ahead of the police boat. We could only gather from the instructions shouted in Dutch, that there was some sort of an emergency situation that had developed further downstream. As the pleasure boats made their exit from the lock, the Police boat rapidly overtook them, and disappeared downstream at high speed.

One hour later, as we rounded a bend in the river, we came across a low flying helicopter which promptly 'buzzed' us every time that we tried to proceed forward. Several times, the down draft from its rotors almost blew my cap off. Clearly, we were being told to stay where we were. In the distance, we could see a large barge that was stationary, and lying at an angle across the channel. On board, and all around the barge, there was a lot of activity. After half an hour of waiting in midstream, we saw a line of pleasure boats coming slowly towards us, hugging the wrong side of the channel. As the first of the Dutch boats passed us, we were told that someone had fallen overboard from the barge and that divers were trying to locate the body. With our engines barely ticking over, we dutifully hugged the right hand bank and crept by the sad and sombre scene.

After an overnight stop at the remote yacht harbour in Kerkdriel, and a magnificent breakfast of pancakes, bacon and sausages, we were well fortified to tackle anything that the busy River Waal might throw at us.

The passage from the River Maas to the River Waal, was made through the short connecting canal and lock of St. Andries. Once we were on the River Waal, we began to appreciate the amount of traffic that the river carries. Further upstream, the Waal later becomes the mighty Rhine, and continues into Germany for 851 kilometres to the limit of navigation at Rheinfelden on the German/Swiss border. In bumpy, windy conditions, we joined the multitude of barges hurrying along the Waal in both directions. Even with our top speed of 12.5 knots we were no match for the powerful Rhine barges and it was necessary to keep a sharp lookout, both ahead and astern.

The Merwede Yacht Club, on the outskirts of Gorinchem, afforded us a calm mooring out of the wind as it was protected on three sides by high dykes. It was not until we walked along the top of the dyke on our way into town that we realized just how much of a wind there was blowing up the river that day. While we were in Gorinchem, Antoinette and Sasha located a laundromat that would get our accumulated piles of washing done much quicker than our little machine on board the boat. An English gentleman at the laundromat, helped in translating the instructions for operating the various machines, which, naturally enough, were in Dutch. Upon finding out that the ladies were from Bermuda his eyes lit up with interest. He told them that his son had recently left England to teach Spanish in Bermuda, and, as so often happens in this small world, it turned out that the gentleman's son was the Spanish teacher of Sasha's youngest son. He accepted their invitation to come on board the boat for a drink that evening, and we thoroughly enjoyed his visit. We were happy to be able to give him some first hand knowledge about Bermuda, and of the school at which his son was teaching.

We left Gorinchem the next day, and made the trip to Gouda in just under five hours and moored up in the centre of the city. Gouda is another Dutch city which has an interesting and varied history, and although it is probably best known for its famous cheese, we found that the city has much more to offer. For me, at least, the stained glass windows in the church of St. John were both remarkable and beautiful. The first of the windows was installed in 1555. The windows were exquisitely and artistically manufactured, and produce an almost three dimensional effect. Among the other treasures that the church has to offer is a Carillon cast by the famous seventeenth century bell founders, the Hermony brothers. It consists of forty-nine bells, many of which are the original ones, cast by Petrus Hemony in 1676. The Carillon has been automated and plays a tune every quarter of an hour. On market days, Thursdays and Saturdays, it is played by the town *carilloneur*.

During our brief stay in Gouda we could explore but a few of the many attractions in this compact and beautiful city. We were already running out of time to make our scheduled arrival in Muiden on 2 September. Our intended route would take us along the Hollandse Ijssel canal, and we had no knowledge of what to expect on this canal in the way of commercial traffic or suitable overnight moorings.

At first, we had some reservations about including the Hollandse Ijssel canal on our itinerary, but after leaving Gouda on September 1st, it soon became apparent that this canal, was both beautiful and convenient. With absolutely no barge traffic to worry about, and very few locks, we made good time and by late afternoon we had covered more than half the total distance of the forty-kilometre canal. We stopped for the night in the small town of Oudewater, and our guests

Along the peaceful Hollandse Ijssel Canal.

returned to the boat later in the evening, with a large oil painting which they had purchased as a souvenir of their Dutch cruise. We dined in a small restaurant where the food was good, but the table service was excruciatingly slow. The waitress seemed more interested in the members of the local football club who were drinking at the bar, than four hungry tourists.

As we passed through Nieuwegan the next day, we left the peaceful Holandse Ijssel canal behind us, and joined in the mayhem on the Amsterdam–Rijn canal. We were being tossed around so much by the wakes of the large, fast-moving barges, that I eventually resorted to switching on the automatic stabilizers which we had not used in two years of cruising. The *Bermuda II* immediately flattened out, and like a greyhound seeking the finish line, raced over the remaining fifteen kilometres with our tattered and faded Bermuda flag on the aft flag pole snapping and cracking in the wind as if urging us on. At the town of Weesp, we turned off the canal to the more gentle waters of the River Vecht.

We approached the lock at Muiden with mixed feelings. Images of white Charollais cattle in emerald green fields, châteaux with round turreted roofs of black slate, misty river mornings, tree shaded canals and a kaleidoscope of faces danced before my eyes. I knew that our extended cruising days were over, and that the *Bermuda II*, which had served us so faithfully would soon find a new owner. I knew also, as much as I might not like it, that it was time to get back to the 'real' world. I also knew that whatever happened, the memories of the places, and the people that we had met over the past two years, were ours to remember forever.

EPILOGUE

So what did we accomplish? Five thousand kilometres and 949 locks—very dull statistics which do not add up to a remarkable feat of inland navigation. To be woken up in the morning by the sun, and not by an alarm clock, and to go to bed by the moon and not the eleven o'clock news was a novel and relaxing lifestyle. The cathedrals and museums will be there for all to see in the future, and the restaurants will continue to serve their fine foods. The beautiful undulating acres of soft purple lavender, fields of bright yellow rape and impressive vine covered slopes, may change a little at the progressive whim of man. Deep down within me, I know that there is more, much more.

Looking through the mental images in my mind, images whose clarity is fading like old photographs washed with age, I can clearly remember the many acts of kindness that were bestowed upon us during our travels. It is, therefore, the wonderful people that we met along the way that create the lasting impressions. Historic buildings, beautiful scenery and quiet canalside and river moorings are but a garnish to the rich fabric of people that interwove with our lives and I hope that we gave of ourselves in the same manner as others gave to us.

We now have a better understanding and respect for the different people who live in different lands, with different customs and different languages. This, together with the realization of a life-long ambition, was our accomplishment.

At the time of writing, the *Bermuda II* has been sold, and we wish her new owners many happy years of cruising on her. Antoinette and I, at some time in the future, would like to purchase a steel hulled craft specifically designed for inland cruising in France. A small barge or a converted *tjalk* would be ideal. We hope, that if all goes well, we can spend several months of each year exploring the canals from which we were excluded due to the size of the *Bermuda II*. The winds of change are blowing through the inland waterways of Europe. It is not a cold wind but a warm wind of opportunity for pleasure craft. Existing moorings and facilities are being improved and new ones are being developed. In due course of time we will return. There is so much to see and do.

The dream begins—again!

December 1994.
Bermuda.

BIBLIOGRAPHY

ANWB. *Almanak Voor Watertoerisme*, Vols I, II. 1991. Koninklijke Nederlandse Toetistenbond.

ANWB. *Waterkaarts*. I. *Vechtplassen*. K. *Grote Rivieren Middenblad*. L. *Grote Rivieren Oostblad*. M. *Limburgse Maas*.

Ardagh, John. *The Collins Guide to France*. (Guild Publishing. London). 1985.

Bazin, Jean-François. *Wonderful Burgundy*. (Editions Ouest France). 1988.

Cole, Robert. *A Traveller's History of France*. (The Windrush Press. London). 1988.

Delpal, Jacques-Louis. *France*. (Phaidon Press Limited, Oxford). 1990.

Edwards-May, David. *Inland Waterways of France* (Imray, St Ives, 1991).

Gombrich, E. H. *Story of Art*. (Phaidon Press Limited, Oxford). 1989.

Hamilton, Ronald. *A Holiday History of France*. (Hogarth Press. London). 1989.

Hogg, Anthony. *Everybody's Wine Guide*. (Quiller Press Limited, London). 1985.

McKnight, Hugh. *Cruising French Waterways*. (Adlard Coles Nautical, London) 1991. *Slow Boat Through France*. (David & Charles. Newton Abbot). 1991.

Michelin Guide Verts—Burgundy. (Michelin, Clermont Ferrand. 1990).

Michelin Guide—France. (Michelin, Clermont Ferrand. 1990).

Sandrin, Michel. *Editions Cartographiques Maritimes*, Joinville le Pont. 2. Seine, Paris-Marcilly. 3. La Marne, Paris Vitry-le-François. 4. Yonne, Auxerre-Montereau. 6. Canaux du Centre, St Mammès-Chalon-sur-Saône. 8. Champagne-Ardenne, Namur-Bourgogne. 10. Saône, Corre-Lyon. 15. Oisne-Aisne Ardenne, Pont-a-Bar-Compiègne. Conflans St Honorine-Conde sur Marne. 16. Rhône, Lyon-Mediterranean. 24. Picardie. 26. Canal de l'Est, Liège-Corre.

Sandrin, Michel & Pigeolet, M. 23. Belgium.

All of the above nautical titles are available by mail order through:
Shepperton Swan Ltd, The Clock House, Upper Halliford, Shepperton, Middlesex, TW17 8EU, England.

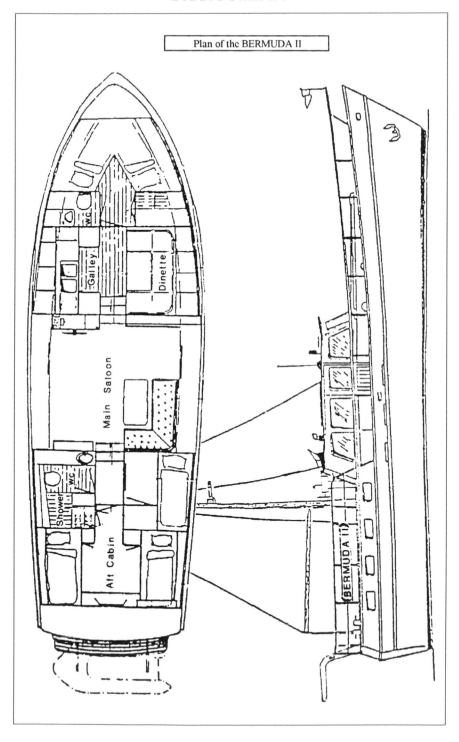

Plan of the BERMUDA II

THE BOURBONNAIS ROUTE
PARIS TO CHALON-SUR-SAÔNE
VIA THE CANALS OF THE CENTRE

Total distance: 447 kilometres
Number of locks: 156

This is not a complete list of suitable moorings. Only those that were used by the *Bermuda II* are listed. All moorings have a minimum water depth of 1.25 metres unless shown otherwise.

Locks, Stops and Shops

Paris Arsenal

All facilities. Reservations advisable in summer months.
Tel: (33) 43 41 39 32 (English spoken).
45.5km 4 locks   to:

St. Fargeau-Ponthierry

Disused lock. No boat facilities.
32.5km 2 locks   to:

Port Stéphane Mallarmé

Water, electricity, garbage disposal. No shops.
16km 1 lock   to:

St. Mammés

Busy commercial port. Mooring possible LHS on approach to

Canal du Loing. Small shops and restaurant five minutes walk.
2.5km 2 locks   to:

Bourgogne

Moorings LHS 100 metres after passing through Lock 18
(Bourgogne). No boat facilities. Town of Moret sur Loing 600
metres. All shops and restaurants.
16.8km 5 locks   to:

Nemours

Good wall with bollards RHS 400 metres after passing through
Lock 12 (Buttes). No boat facilities. All shops and restaurants ten
minutes walk. Pleasure port on River Loing embranchment before
Lock 12. Max. draught 1.2 metres. Pontoons, water, electricity,
garbage disposal, public telephone. All shops and restaurants five
minutes walk.
27km 9 locks to:

Cépoy

Moorings RHS 50 metres before Lock 1 (Cépoy). Some sloping
stone walls. Water, electricity, garbage disposal, public telephone.
Small shops 100 metres.
5.5km 3 locks   to:

Montargis

Quay with bollards LHS fifty metres before N7 road bridge. No
boat facilities. Water tap LHS at upper end of commercial port. All
shops and restaurants five minutes walk. Moorings also available
RHS fifty metres after passing through Lock 33 (La Marolle).
5.1km 2 locks   to:

Tuilerie

Good quay with bollards RHS 200 Metres before Lock 32 (Tuilerie).
15.8km 7 locks   to:

Montbouy

New facility LHS 200 metres after Lock 26 (Montbuoy). Water,
electricity, garbage disposal. Small shops 400 metres.
5.6km 1 lock   to:

Châtillon Coligny

Moorings RHS 200 metres before Lock 24 (Châtillon). Water, electricity, garbage disposal. Small shops.

10.1km 7 locks   to:

Rogny

Good quay with bollards LHS 200 metres before Lock 18 (Ste. Barbe). Water. Pleasure port LHS immediately before Lock 18. Water, electricity, showers, toilets, garbage disposal, public telephone. Small supermarket and restaurants five minutes walk. Of interest: Seven ancient lock chambers (c.1642) now preserved as a national monument.

16.2km 14 locks   to:

Briare

Mooring basin. Quay RHS immediately before aqueduct. Water on quay under metal hinged plate, garbage disposal, public telephone. All shops and restaurants 300 metres. Pleasure port 1.5km down embranchment canal (3 Locks). Max draught 1.2 metres. Water, electricity, public telephone, garbage disposal. All shops, restaurants, supermarket and laundrette in immediate area. Of Interest: Briare aquaduct designed by M. Eiffel. Extensive antique car and motor cycle museum fifteen minutes cycle ride on N7 road. Enquire at Tourist Office in town centre as to hours of opening.

6.2km 0 locks   to:

Châtillon sur Loire

Mooring possible RHS alongside sloping stone walls. Water, electricity, garbage disposal, public telephone. Small shops five minutes walk.

12km 1 lock   to:

Belleville

Excellent quay with bollards RHS before Lock 37 (Belleville). Water, electricity, garbage disposal. Small shops. Also good quay with bollards LHS 100 metres after Lock 37.

4.2km 1 lock   to:

Léré

Small pleasure port of uncertain depth. Good mooring RHS fifty metres before pleasure port. Water. Small shops five minutes walk.
10km 3 locks   to:

Bannay

Quay RHS immediately in front of Hôtel La Bussonière. Water, Electricity, garbage disposal. Restaurant across road.
5.8km 0 locks   to:

St. Thibault

Moorings on branch canal mainly alongside sloping stone walls. Water, garbage disposal, public telephone, bakery. Supermarket 1km. Restaurants five minutes walk. Town of Sancerre 2km uphill. All shops and restaurants. Of Interest: Town of Sancerre famous for its wine. Fiefs Tower. Panoramic view overlooking Loire valley. Restaurant Saint-Roch (Two converted *berrichon* barges) on River Loire.
2.6km 0 locks   to:

Ménetréol

Moorings RHS with sloping stone walls. Water, electricity, garbage disposal, public telephone. Small shops. Sancerre 2.5km uphill.
14km 3 locks   to:

Herry

Quay with bollards RHS 200 metres before Lock 30 (Herry). No boat facilities. Small shops five minutes walk.
22.4km 6 locks   to:

Cours les Barres. (Near)

Moorings RHS with bollards. English book exchange.
10.1km 1 lock   to:

Le Guétin

Quay with bollards RHS before Locks 21/22 double staircase. No water. Small shop ten minute walk.
7.8km 2 locks   to:

Plagny

Pleasure port RHS. Water, garbage disposal, public telephone. Baker but no other shops.

22.2km 3 locks   to:

Fleury sur Loire

Quay with bollards RHS after Lock 18 (Fleury). Water.

12km 2 locks   to:

Decize

Mooring possible LHS immediately before branch canal, or through two locks on branch canal and then 500 metres downstream RHS just after distinctive road bridge over River Loire. Water, garbage disposal. Large supermarket 100 metres. All shops and restaurants ten minutes walk. Pleasure port an additional 500 metres downstream. Pontoons, water, electricity, garbage disposal. All shops and restaurants fifteen minutes walk.

16.2km 4 locks   to:

Gannay sur Loire

Moorings RHS immediately after Lock 12 (Vanneaux). Water. Small shops 1km. Hire boat base.

11.6km 2 locks   to:

Garnat sur Engievre

Pontoons RHS immediately after road bridge. Water, garbage disposal.

3km 1 lock   to:

Beaulon

Quay with bollards RHS before Lock 8 (Beaulon). No boat facilities.

12.2km 3 locks   to:

Diou

Good quay LHS with bollards and mooring rings. Water, garbage disposal, public telephone. Small supermarket fifty metres. Restaurant. Craft exceeding 1.3 metres draught should approach

quay with caution.
6.4km 2 locks   to:

Pierrefitte sur Loire

Pleasure port RHS. Water, garbage disposal. Small shops ten minutes cycle ride. Bar/restaurant alongside canal.
4.2km 1 lock   to:

Coulanges

New facility LHS. Untried.
6.9km 1 lock   to:

Molinet

New facility RHS. Water. No shops in immediate vicinity.
3.9km 1 lock   to:

Digoin

Pleasure port RHS. Moorings alongside corrugations before road bridge or alongside pontoons RHS after bridge. Water, electricity, showers, garbage disposal, public telephone. All shops and restaurants five minutes walk.
12.8km 3 locks   to:

Paray le Monial

Tree shaded moorings LHS before main road bridge. No water. All shops and large supermarket five minutes walk. Numerous restaurants. Of Interest: Basilica of the Holy Heart. Parc des Chapelains.
19.8km 7 locks   to:

Génelard

Quay with bollards RHS before Lock 16 (Génelard). Water tap on end of navigation authority warehouse. Also possible to moor LHS immediately before Lock 16 alongside grassed bank. Small shops ten minutes walk. Good restaurant overlooking lock and canal.
17.6km 7 locks   to:

Montceau-les-Mines

Moorings for pleasure boats limited to a small area in turning basin RHS after lifting bridge. No water. All shops and restaurants

five minutes walk. Pleasure port planned for 1994/5. Additional moorings on outskirts of town LHS after Lock 10 (Chavannes). No water. All shops and restaurants fifteen minutes walk.
11.7km 9 locks   to:

Montchanin

Mooring may be permitted for short time only and upon request at hire boat basin RHS after Lock 1 (Ocean). All shops and restaurants fifteen minutes cycle ride.
19.5km 19 locks   to:

St. Léger-sur-Dheune

Pleasure port RHS before bridge. Water, electricity, garbage disposal, petrol, diesel (ask at lumber yard office), public telephone. Small shops and restaurant 200 metres. Large supermarket RHS 500 metres on main road leading to railway station.
11.4km 4 locks   to:

Chagny

Mooring basin. Water only available from LHS. All shops and restaurants ten minutes walk.
19.3km 12 locks   to:

Chalon-sur-Saône

Extensive Marina. Water, electricity, showers, toilets, garbage disposal, small crane, petrol, public telephone. Large supermarket 200 metres from port. All shops and restaurants five minutes walk. Recommended: Le Gourmand and L'Eau du Bouche both on the Ile St Laurent. Of Interest: Comprehensive photography museum, Nicéphore Niepce, on the Quai Gambretta. St Vincent's Cathedral and various other historic buildings.

N.B. All of the above moorings were used by the *Bermuda II* but neither the author nor publisher can be held responsible for any accident or damage arising from the use of this information.

Canal de la Marne a la Saône From Vitry-le-François to Maxilly sur Saône

Total distance: 224.2 Kilometres
Number of locks: 114

This is not a complete list of suitable moorings. Only those that were used by the *Bermuda II* are listed. All moorings have a minimum water depth of 1.25 metres.

Locks, Stops and Shops

Vitry-le-François

Small Pleasure port. Water, electricity, garbage disposal. Petrol and diesel available from fuel barge on Canal latéral à la Marne. Some chandlery on barge. Large town. All shops and restaurants.
28.2km 12 locks to:

St. Dizier

Small pleasure port immediately before Lock 59 (La Noue). Water, electricity, garbage disposal, some chandlery. Small shops 400 metres. Large town 800 metres. All shops and restaurants.
56.2km 24 locks to:

Froncles

Mooring RHS after Lock 36 (Froncles). No boat facilities. Small

shops and supermarket 500 metres.
25.6km 11 locks   to:

Chaumont

Moorings between Locks 25 (Relancourt) and Lock 24 (Val de Choux). No boat facilities. Large town 1km. All shops and restaurants.
14.3km 8 locks   to:

Foulain

Mooring possible LHS after Lock 17 (Foulain). No boat facilities. Also mooring possible alongside grass banks LHS after road bridge. No boat facilities. Small shops 800 metres.
24.5km 14 locks   to:

Langres

Quay RHS after Lock 3 (Moulin Rouge). No boat facilities. Large town 1.5km (uphill). All shops and restaurants.
12.9km 2 locks   to:

Heuilley Cotton

Mooring possible LHS alongside grass banks. No boat facilities. Small shops 500 metres.
5.8km 8 locks   to:

Villegusien

Quay LHS after road bridge. No boat facilities. Small shops 600 metres.
12.7km 13 locks   to:

Cusey

Mooring possible against LHS corrugations after Lock 21 (Montrepelle). No boat facilities. Small shops 1.5km.
34.2km 18 locks   to:

Renève

Quay RHS after Lock 39 (Rèneve) downstream of road bridge. No boat facilities. Small shops 500 metres.
8.3km 2 locks   to:

Maxilly sur Saône

Quay RHS before Lock 42 (Maxilly). No boat facilities. Small shops 1.5km

N.B. All of the above moorings were used by the *Bermuda II* but neither the author nor publisher can take responsibility for any accident or damage arising from the use of this information.

St. Jean-de-Losne to Avignon via the River Saône and the River Rhône

Total distance: 433.9 kilometres
Number of locks: 16

This is not a complete list of all suitable mooring places, but these have all been tried and found suitable for a craft of 1.25 metres draught.

St. Jean-de-Losne

Large pleasure port operated by company H_2O. Also berths available at marina run by Ets. Blanquart both located in the Gare d'eau. Entrance to the Gare d'eau is on RHS immediately in front of the first lock on the Canal de Bourgogne. Water, electricity, showers, laundromat, public telephone. garbage disposal, repairs. All shops and supermarket 200 Metres.
15.5km 1 lock   to:

Seurre

Moorings LHS after Lock 7 (Seurre). Water, garbage disposal, public telephone. All shops and restaurants 200 metres.
43.5km 1 lock   to:

Chalon-sur-Saône

Large pleasure port. (See Bourbannais route for Notes).
73.3km 1 lock   to:

Tournus

Quay RHS after road bridge, or if less than 1.25 metres draught alongside quay RHS upstream of road bridge. Water, garbage disposal. All shops and restaurants 200 metres. Of interest: eleventh-century Abbey of St. Philibert.
28.9km 0 locks   to:

Mâcon

Pleasure port RHS before city. Water, electricity, garbage disposal, public telephone. Shops and restaurants 2km or continue downstream 2.7km to quay with sloping sides RHS after road bridge. Water. All shops and restaurants in immediate vicinity.
19.7km 0 locks   to:

Thoissey

Quay RHS. No boat facilities.
32.7km 1 lock   to:

Trevoux

Quay RHS before road bridge. No boat facilities. Small shops and restaurants 100 metres.
27km 1 lock   to:

Lyon

Quay LHS between footbridge and Pont Bonaparte. Garbage disposal. All shops and restaurants in immediate area. Daily produce market (mornings) along Quai St. Antoine.
32.5km 1 lock   to:

Vienne

Quay LHS after road bridge. No boat facilities. All shops and restaurants fifty metres.
11.1km 1 lock   to:

Les Roches des Condrieu

Pleasure port LHS. Water, electricity, garbage disposal, public telephone. Small shops and restaurant 100 metres.
48.3km 2 locks   to:

Tournon

Small pleasure port RHS. Water, electricity, garbage disposal, public telephone. Small shops and restaurants in immediate area.
21km 1 lock   to:

Valence

Large pleasure port RHS 2km downstream from main town at PK112. Entrance through buoyed channel. Water, electricity, garbage disposal, public telephone, laundromat, chandlery shop. Restaurant. Large supermarket 800 metres. All shops and restaurants 2.5km (Bus service).
46.5km 2 locks   to:

Montélimar

Quay LHS but may be taken up with commercial craft. No boat facilities.
26.6km 1 lock   to:

Bollène

Quay RHS 500 metres upstream of lock. No boat facilities.
34.1km 2 locks   to:

Roquemaure

Quay RHS. No boat facilities. Small shops and restaurants 500 metres. Very dangerous at time of mistral. Totally unprotected.
14.4km 1 lock   to:

Avignon

Pleasure port 2.5km upstream on River Durance. Water, electricity, garbage disposal, public telephone, showers, petrol, diesel. All shops and restaurants 300 metres. Of Interest: Pope's Palace. Pont St Benezet.

NB. All moorings mentioned above were tried by the *Bermuda II* but neither the author nor publisher can be held responsible for any accident or damage arising from the use of this information.

INDEX

229